ProMgmt.

Principles of Food, Beverage, and Labor Cost Controls

SEVENTH EDITION

Student Workbook

National Restaurant Association
EDUCATIONAL FOUNDATION

JOHN WILEY & SONS, INC.

Library of Congress Cataloging-in-Publication Data:

ISBN: 0-471-20877-9

Printed in the United States of America

10 9 8 7 6 5 4 3 2

CONTENTS

INTRODUCTION

Cost monitoring and cost control are indispensable components of a successful foodservice and hospitality manager's skill set. *Principles of Food, Beverage, and Labor Cost Control, Seventh Edition,* prepares students entering the hospitality workforce by helping them develop crucial financial management skills.

This course offers an introduction to food, beverage, and labor cost controls, including definitions of key terms and the basics of cost-volume-profit analysis. It also focuses on controlling purchasing, receiving, storing, and issuing, exploring specific techniques and procedures for each topic.

The ProMgmt.® Program

How to Earn a ProMgmt. Certificate of Course Completion

To earn a ProMgmt. Certificate of Course Completion, a student must complete all student workbook exercises and receive a passing score on the final examination.

To apply for the ProMgmt. Certificate of Course Completion, complete the student registration form located on the inside back cover of this workbook and give it to your instructor, who will then forward it to the National Restaurant Association Educational Foundation.

Each student registered with the NRAEF will receive a student number. Please make a record of it; this number will identify you during your present and future coursework with the NRAEF.

ProMgmt. certificate requirements are administered exclusively through colleges and other educational institutions that offer ProMgmt. courses and examinations.

If you are not currently enrolled in a ProMgmt. course and would like to earn a ProMgmt. certificate, please contact your local educational institution to see if they are willing to administer the ProMgmt. certificate requirements for non-enrolled students. You can also visit www.nraef.org for a list of ProMgmt. Partner schools. ProMgmt. Partner schools offer seven or more courses that include administration of the ProMgmt. certificate requirements.

The NRAEF leaves it to the discretion of each educational institution offering ProMgmt. courses to decide whether or not that institution will administer the ProMgmt. certificate requirements to non-enrolled students. If an institution does administer ProMgmt. certificate requirements to non-enrolled students, that institution may charge an additional fee, of an amount determined by that institution, for the administration of the ProMgmt. certificate requirements.

Course Materials

This course consists of the text, *Principles of Food, Beverage, and Labor Cost Controls, Seventh Edition,* by Paul R. Dittmer, the student workbook, and a final examination. The examination is the final section of your course and is sent to an instructor for administration, then returned to the NRAEF for grading.

Each chapter consists of:
- Learning Objectives
- Chapter Study Outline
- Chapter Check-in
- Answers to Chapter Check-in (at the end of the workbook)

At the end of the workbook you will find:
- An 80-question practice test
- Answers to the practice test

The objectives indicate what you can expect to learn from the course, and are designed to help you organize your studying and concentrate on important topics and explanations. Refer to the objectives frequently to make sure you are meeting them.

The exercises help you check how well you've learned the concepts in each chapter. These will be graded by your instructor.

An 80-question Practice Test appears at the end of the workbook. All the questions are multiple-choice and have four possible answers. Circle the best answer to each question, as in this example:

Who was the first president of the United States?
A. Thomas Jefferson
B. *George Washington*
C. Benjamin Franklin
D. John Adams

Answers to the Practice Test follow in the workbook so that you can grade your own work.

The Final Exam

All examinations can first be graded by your instructor and then officially graded again by the NRAEF. If you do not receive a passing grade on the examination, you may request a retest. A retest fee will be charged for the second examination.

Study Tips

Since you have already demonstrated an interest in furthering your foodservice education by registering for this NRAEF course, you know that your next step is study preparation. We have included some specific study aids that you might find useful.

-   Build studying time into your routine. If you hold a full-time job, you need to take a realistic approach to studying. Set aside a specific time and place to study, and stick to your routine as closely as possible. Your study area should have room for your course materials and any other necessary study aids. If possible, your area should be away from family traffic.
-   Discuss with family members your study goals and your need for a quiet place and private time to work. They might want to help you draw up a study schedule that will be satisfactory to everyone.
-   Keep a study log. You can record what chapter was worked on, a list of topics studied, the time you put in, and how well you scored on the Chapter Check-ins and Practice Text.
-   Work at your own pace, but move ahead steadily. The following tips should help you get the most value from your lessons.
    1. Look over the objectives carefully. They list what you are expected to know for the examination.

2. Read the chapters carefully, and don't hesitate to mark your text—it will help you later. Mark passages that seem especially important and those that seem difficult, as you might want to reread them later.
3. Try to read an entire chapter at a time. Even though more than one chapter might be assigned at time, you might find you can carefully read only one chapter in a sitting.
4. When you have finished reading the chapter, go back and check the highlights and any notes you have made. These will help you review for the examination.

Reviewing for the Final Exam

Once you have completed the final exercise and Practice Test, you will have several items to use for your examination review. If you have highlighted important points in the textbook, you can review them. If you have made notes in the margins, check them to be sure you have answered any questions that arose when you read the material. Reread certain sections if necessary. Finally, you should go over your exercises.

The ProMgmt.® Program

The National Restaurant Association Educational Foundation's ProMgmt. program is designed to provide foodservice students and professionals with a solid foundation of practical knowledge and information. Each course focuses on a specific management area. Students who earn ProMgmt. certificates improve their chances of:
-    Earning NRAEF Undergraduate Scholarships.
-    Gaining management jobs within the foodservice and restaurant industry.

For more information on both the ProMgmt. program and scholarships, please contact the NRAEF at 800.765.2122 (312.715.1010 in Chicagoland), or visit our Web site at **www.nraef.org**.

CHAPTER 1

Learning Objectives

1.1   Define the terms *cost* and *sales*.

1.2   Define and provide an example of the following types of costs: fixed, directly variable, semivariable, controllable, noncontrollable, unit, total, prime, historical, and planned.

1.3   Provide several examples illustrating monetary and nonmonetary sales concepts.

1.4   Describe the significance of cost-to-sales relationships and identify several cost-to-sales ratios important in food and beverage management.

1.5   Identify the formulas used to compute the following: cost percent, sales price, maximum allowable cost per person.

1.6   Describe factors that cause industry-wide variations in cost percent.

1.7   Explain the value of comparing current cost-to-sales ratios with those for previous periods.

Chapter 1 Study Outline

1. Cost is the expense to a hotel or restaurant of goods or services when the goods are consumed or the services rendered.
2. Costs can be classified in a variety of ways.
    - Fixed costs are unaffected by changes in sales volume. Variable costs are directly related to business volume.
    - Payroll costs are semivariable since they have both a fixed and a variable element.
    - Controllable costs can be changed in the short term, while noncontrollable costs cannot.
    - Prime costs refer to the costs of materials and labor: food, beverages, and payroll.
    - Historical costs are found in business records and are used to develop planned costs.

1

3. Sales are the revenue resulting from the exchange of products and services for value.

- Sales can be expressed in both monetary and nonmonetary terms.
- Managers need to be continually aware of costs and keep costs below the level of sales.

4. The formula for calculating cost-to-sales ratio is Cost ÷ Sales = Cost per dollar of sale.

- The formula can be extended to show food cost percent, beverage cost percent, and labor cost percent.
- Cost percents provide a means of comparing both the costs relative to sales for two or more periods of time and the costs of two or more similar operations.
- The cost percent formula can be rearranged algebraically to facilitate other calculations. The calculation of a sales price is simplified if the formula is rearranged in the following form: Cost ÷ Cost percent = Sales (Sales price).
- The calculation of cost is facilitated by rearranging the formula once again: Sales ÷ Cost percent = Cost.

5. Cost percentages vary considerably from one foodservice operation to another.

Chapter 1 Exercises

The controller of the Harvest Restaurant has been supplied with the following year-end cost information.

___	a.	Administrative expenses	$2,430
___	b.	Employee benefits (40% fixed)	$24,750
___	c.	Cost of food sold	$110,580
___	d.	Salaries and wages (40% fixed)	$111,400
___	e.	Utilities	$23,470
___	f.	Depreciation on equipment	$14,400
___	g.	Cost of beverages sold	$13,790
___	h.	Interest expense	$2,550
___	i.	Occupancy costs	$32,550
___	j.	Advertising	$3,700

1. Identify each of the costs above as fixed (F), variable (V), or semivariable (S).
L.O. 1.1, 1.2

2. Given that food sales were $350,000 for the year and beverage sales $55,800, prepare a statement of income on a separate sheet of paper for the Harvest Restaurant. (Use Figure 1.1 on text page 5 as a guide.) Include advertising, utilities, and administrative expenses as one lump sum under *Other Controllable Expenses*. Did the Harvest Restaurant make a profit?

_____

L.O. 1.1

3. Based on the figures above, calculate the Harvest Restaurant's:
   _____a. Prime cost
   _____b. Food cost percent
   _____c. Beverage cost percent
   _____d. Labor cost percent

L.O. 1.2, 1.4, 1.5

4. Identify each of the following sales concepts as monetary (M) or nonmonetary (N).

_____a. Sales price	_____d. Total sales per server
_____b. Cover	_____e. Seat turnover
_____c. Sales mix	_____f. Average sale

L.O. 1.3

5. The Harvest Restaurant features ten menu items. Calculate the sales mix for the last month given the information below. Do not round off percentages.

Menu Item	Portion Sales	Sales Mix %
1	500	
2	600	
3	900	
4	1,200	
5	800	
6	550	
7	1,000	
8	950	
9	850	
10	650	
Totals		

L.O. 1.3

6. Why might the Harvest Restaurant's cost percents differ significantly from those of other foodservice operations?

_____

_____

_____

L.O. 1.6

7. Why should the Harvest Restaurant's cost controller compare current cost-to-sales ratios to those for previous periods?

_____

_____

_____

L.O. 1.7

Chapter 1 Check-in

1. The cost of labor is incurred when employees are

   A. hired.
   B. discharged.
   C. on duty.
   D. off duty.

   L.O. 1.1

2. Which of the following statements is true about fixed costs?

   A. They include a semivariable component.
   B. They change over time.
   C. They are directly linked to volume of business.
   D. They include utility, rent, food, beverage, and labor costs.

   L.O. 1.2

3. Costs that can be changed in the short term are called

   A. controllable costs.
   B. unit costs.
   C. total costs.
   D. overhead costs.

   L.O. 1.2

4. Food, beverage, and payroll costs are collectively known as

   A. historical cost.
   B. planned cost.
   C. prime cost.
   D. variable cost.

   L.O. 1.2

5. If Alice's total dollar sales were $500 last Tuesday and she served 32 customers, her average sale was

   A. $10.80.
   B. $12.38.
   C. $14.33.
   D. $15.63.

   L.O. 1.3

6. If the Sugar Plum served 300 people in a dining room with 125 seats, what was the establishment's seat turnover for the period?

    A. 2.2
    B. 2.4
    C. 2.8
    D. 3.1

L.O. 1.3

7. Which of the following can be used to calculate cost per dollar of sale?

    A. Cost ÷ Sales
    B. Sales ÷ Cost
    C. Cost ÷ Cost percentage
    D. Sales × Cost percentage

L.O. 1.4

8. What would be an appropriate menu price for a veal marsala entree if the cost percent is 26.1% and the food cost for the item is $4.10?

    A. $15.75
    B. $16.95
    C. $17.99
    D. $19.99

L.O. 1.5

9. In general, foodservice establishments that operate at relatively high margins of profit per item

    A. require high business volume.
    B. have higher labor cost and lower food cost percent.
    C. employ unskilled personnel.
    D. have higher food cost percents than quick-service establishments.

L.O. 1.6

10. When calculating current cost-to-sales ratios, the data should be

    A. calculated in fraction form.
    B. verified by the company accountant.
    C. converted into decimal form.
    D. from like periods.

L.O. 1.7

CHAPTER 2

Learning Objectives

2.1 Define *control* and provide examples of its significance in food and beverage management.

2.2 Pinpoint responsibility for control in a food and beverage operation.

2.3 Cite eight control techniques used in food and beverage operations.

2.4 Describe the steps involved in preparing an operating budget.

2.5 List the four steps in the control process.

2.6 Explain why the cost-benefit ratio is significant when making control decisions.

Chapter 2 Study Outline

1. Cost control is the process used by managers to regulate costs and guard against excessive costs; sales control ensures that all sales result in appropriate income to the business.

2. Responsibility for every aspect of a food and beverage operation rests with management.

3. The control techniques available to a manager include the following:
   - Establishing standards, such as quality, quantity, and costs
   - Establishing procedures, including standard procedures
   - Training employees
   - Setting examples
   - Observing and correcting employee actions
   - Requiring records and reports, such as statements of income
   - Disciplining employees
   - Preparing and following budgets, such as operating budgets

6

4. The steps in preparing an operating budget are:
   - Examine sales figures from the recent past to note evident trends.
   - Examine the external environment and assess any conditions or factors that could affect sales volume in the coming year. These usually include general economic conditions in the nation and in the immediate geographical area, population changes, or changes that might affect transportation to the establishment.
   - Review any planned changes in the operation that would affect sales volume, such as changing menu prices.
   - Determine the nature and extent of changes in cost levels, some of which will be dictated by anticipated changes in sales volume and others that will occur independent of volume changes.
   - Give completed projections of sales, costs, and profits to management, who must accept and adopt them as the plan of action for the covered period. Once accepted, an operating budget becomes a standard against which operating performance is measured as the fiscal year progresses.
   - Counteract the inherent shortcomings of fixed operating budgets. A manager can prepare a budget designed to project sales and costs for several levels of business activity—a flexible budget.
5. The control process consists of four steps:
   - Establish standards and standard procedures for operation.
   - Train all individuals to follow established standards and standard procedures.
   - Monitor performance and compare actual performance to established standards.
   - Take appropriate action to correct deviations from standards, or change the standard if it is unrealistic or inappropriate.
6. A control system is a collection of interrelated and interdependent control techniques and procedures.
7. The cost/benefit ratio is the relationship between the costs incurred in instituting and maintaining a control or control system and the benefits or savings derived by doing so.

Chapter 2 Exercises

1. How do cost control and sales control differ?

   _____

   _____

   _____

L.O. 2.1

2. Who is responsible for control in a foodservice establishment?

   _____

L.O. 2.2

3. For each of the following control techniques, provide an example of how the technique might be applied in a foodservice operation.

   a. Establishing standards

   _____

   b. Establishing procedures

   _____

   c. Training

   _____

   d. Setting examples

   _____

   e. Observing and correcting employee actions

   _____

   f. Requiring records and reports

   _____

   g. Disciplining employees

   _____

   h. Preparing and following budgets

   _____

L.O. 2.3

4. Given the statement of income prepared for the Harvest Restaurant in the Chapter 1 Exercises, create a budget on a separate sheet of paper based on the following anticipated changes:

   a. Food sales are expected to increase by 6%.
   b. Beverage sales are expected to increase by 4%.
   c. Salaries and wages will increase by 3%.
   d. Other controllable costs will increase by $5,900.
   e. Occupancy costs will increase by $3,400.

L.O. 2.4

5. Indicate whether each of the following statements is true (T) or false (F).

_____a. A budget designed to project sales and costs for several levels of business activity is called a static budget.

_____b. The final step of the control process is to monitor performance and compare actual performance to established standards.

_____c. The time required for the savings to pay for the cost of a new procedure is known as the cost/benefit ratio.

_____d. The ratio of cost to benefit should always be less than one.

_____e. The first step of the control process is to establish standards and standard procedures for operation.

_____f. The period of time required for the savings to pay for the cost of a new procedure is known as the payback period.

L.O. 2.4–2.6

Chapter 2 Check-in

1. The goal of cost control is to
   A. eliminate excessive costs for food, beverages, and labor.
   B. establish goals and subgoals compatible with long-range plans.
   C. ensure that all sales result in appropriate income to the business.
   D. outpace the competition.

L.O. 2.1

2. The larger and more complex an establishment, the more likely it is that control procedures will be handled by
   A. management.
   B. subordinates.
   C. auditors.
   D. consultants.

L.O. 2.2

3. Which of the following are used to define the degree of excellence of raw materials, finished products, and employee work?
   A. Standard costs
   B. Quantity standards
   C. Quality standards
   D. Standard procedures

L.O. 2.3

4. In larger operations, management's observations must often be abstracted and inferred from
   A. employee misconduct.
   B. training seminars.
   C. sales control standards.
   D. records and reports.

L. O. 2.3

5. Only if corrective action has failed do managers resort to

   A. committee action.
   B. promotion.
   C. termination.
   D. discipline.

   L.O. 2.3

6. An operating budget is usually prepared using

   A. historical information from previous budgets.
   B. figures from competitors.
   C. static data.
   D. computer-generated cost information.

   L.O. 2.4

7. The second step in the control process is to

   A. take appropriate action to correct deviations from standards.
   B. train all individuals to follow established standards and standard procedures.
   C. establish standards and standard procedures for operation.
   D. compare standards and standard procedures to the establishment's goals and mission statement.

   L.O. 2.5

8. A collection of interrelated and interdependent control techniques is called a

   A. budget.
   B. standard.
   C. control system.
   D. control process.

   L.O. 2.7

9. Which of the following actions is likely to have the shortest payback period?

   A. Relocating the cashier's station to a more suitable position
   B. Installing a closed-circuit television security system
   C. Installing locks for food-storage facilities
   D. Implementing a total quality control system

   L.O. 2.6

10. The ratio of cost to benefit should always be

    A. equal to one.
    B. greater than one.
    C. less than one.
    D. an estimate.

    L.O. 2.6

CHAPTER 3

COST/VOLUME/PROFIT RELATIONSHIPS

Learning Objectives

3.1   State the cost/volume/profit equation and explain the relationships that exist among its components.

3.2   Apply the formulas used to determine: sales in dollars; sales in units; variable costs; fixed costs; profit; contribution rate; contribution margin; variable rate, and break-even point.

Chapter 3 Study Outline

1. The relationships between and among sales, cost of sales, cost of labor, cost of overhead, and profit can be expressed as Sales = Cost of sales + Cost of labor + Cost of overhead + Profit.
    - Because cost of sales is variable, cost of labor includes both fixed and variable elements, and cost of overhead is fixed, the equation can be restated as Sales = Variable cost + Fixed cost + Profit (S = VC + FC + P).
2. Variable rate is the percent of dollar sales needed to cover variable costs. Variable cost ÷ Sales = Variable rate.
    - If part of the sales dollar is used to cover variable costs, then the remainder is available to meet fixed costs and provide profit.
    - Contribution rate = 1 – Variable rate.
3. Break-even occurs when costs equal sales. The following formula can be used to determine the level of dollar sales required to earn any desired profit:

    Fixed cost + Profit ÷ Contribution rate = Sales.
    - This equation determines the break-even point when profit is set equal to 0.
4. Contribution margin = Selling price – Variable costs of that item.
    - The importance of contribution margin in food and beverage management cannot be overemphasized.
    - Any item sold for which variable cost exceeds sales price immediately results in a negative contribution margin.

Chapter 3 Exercises

Use the following cost information for the Austin Grill to answer the questions below. Round all answers to the nearest dollar.

Food cost	$125,750
Variable labor cost	$40,500
Occupancy cost	$37,000
Interest	$13,350
Depreciation	$22,230
Beverage cost	$28,500
Fixed labor cost	$57,050
Other controllable expenses	$51,100

1. What is the establishment's profit if sales are $397,000? What is the basic cost/volume/profit equation?

L.O. 3.1, 3.2

2. What is the variable rate for the Austin Grill? What does this figure mean?

L.O. 3.1, 3.2

3. What is the contribution rate for the Austin Grill? What does this figure mean?

L.O. 3.1, 3.2

4. What is the break-even point for the Austin Grill? What does this figure mean?

_____

_____

_____

L.O. 3.1, 3.2

5. What level of dollar sales is required in order for the Austin Grill to earn a profit of $50,000?

_____

L.O. 3.1, 3.2

6. If the establishment operated at a loss of $25,250 last year, what was its level of dollar sales?

_____

L.O. 3.1, 3.2

7. Calculate the establishment's contribution margin based on the cost/volume/profit values calculated in Question 1.

_____

L.O. 3.2

8. If the manager has not been controlling variable costs and the variable rate rises to 0.552, what sales level is now required to earn the same profit (from Question 1)?

_____

L.O. 3.1, 3.2

Chapter 3 Check-in

1. Lowering contribution margins will require which of the following if a foodservice establishment wants to achieve a given target profit?

   A. Increasing variable cost
   B. Increasing volume
   C. Maintaining break-even levels
   D. Lowering sale prices

   L.O. 3.1

2. If current records of Brady's Bistro show cost of overhead at $80,000, cost of labor at $47,000, cost of sales at $65,000, and profit of $4,500, what is the establishment's total dollar sales?

   A. $175,500
   B. $196,500
   C. $204,500
   D. $211,500

   L.O. 3.2

3. The relationship between variable costs and sales

   A. changes as fixed costs increase and decrease.
   B. mimics the rate of inflation.
   C. remains relatively constant.
   D. is irrelevant to understanding the cost/volume/profit relationship.

   L.O. 3.2

4. For the first quarter of the year, a hotel foodservice operation had fixed costs of $230,000, variable costs of $420,000, and sales of $845,000. What was the operation's variable rate?

   A. .435
   B. .478
   C. .497
   D. .505

   L.O. 3.2

5. If 49.8% of dollar sales is needed to cover the variable costs of Ely's Eatery, what is the establishment's contribution rate?

   A. .498
   B. .502
   C. 49.8
   D. 50.2

   L.O. 3.1, 3.2

6. Last year, the China Inn had fixed costs of $433,300 and variable costs of $345,000. If sales were $925,000, what was the operation's profit?

   A. $94,775
   B. $114,995
   C. $131,545
   D. $146,700

   L.O. 3.2

7. Variable cost can be determined by multiplying sales by

   A. variable rate.
   B. contribution rate.
   C. contribution margin.
   D. fixed cost.

   L.O. 3.1, 3.2

14

8. To determine an establishment's break-even point, which of the following should be set to zero?

    A. Sales
    B. Fixed cost
    C. Profit
    D. Contribution rate

L.O. 3.2

9. Beef burritos sell for $8.95. If the variable cost for the menu item is $6.80, what is the contribution margin for the item?

    A. $1.20
    B. $1.80
    C. $2.00
    D. $2.15

L.O. 3.2

10. An adequate contribution margin will cover fixed costs of an operation and also

    A. take into account semivariable costs.
    B. allow for year-end bonuses and incentives.
    C. provide for an additional amount beyond break-even that equals the desired profit.
    D. result in break-even.

L.O. 3.1, 3.2

15

CHAPTER 4

Learning Objectives

4.1   Describe the application of the four-step control process to the purchasing function in a foodservice establishment.

4.2   List distinguishing characteristics of both perishable and nonperishable foods.

4.3   Describe how quality standards for food purchases are established.

4.4   Describe how quantity standards for perishable and nonperishable food purchases are established.

4.5   List six reasons that standard purchase specifications are important and provide examples of specifications for both a perishable and a nonperishable food item.

4.6   Describe the process used to determine the quantity of perishable foods to be purchased.

4.7   Compare and contrast the periodic order method and perpetual inventory methods for purchasing nonperishable foods.

4.8   Determine order quantities using the periodic order method.

4.9   Determine order quantities using the perpetual inventory method.

4.10   List the normal sources of supply for restaurant food purchases.

4.11   Describe the procedures for purchasing perishable and nonperishable foods at the most favorable prices.

4.12   List five methods for training employees responsible for purchasing foods.

4.13   Outline possible consequences of failure to train employees responsible for purchasing.

4.14   List and explain the advantages and disadvantages of centralized purchasing.

4.15   List and explain the advantages and disadvantages of standing orders.

4.16   Explain several computer applications for food purchasing.

Chapter 4 Study Outline

1. Responsibility for food purchasing can be given to a number of different people—managers, owners, chefs, or stewards. For control purposes, the authority to purchase foods and the responsibility for doing so, however, should be assigned to one individual.

2. Perishable foods have a comparatively short useful life after they have been received, while nonperishables have a longer one.

3. The primary purpose for establishing control over purchasing is to ensure a continuing supply of sufficient quantities of necessary foods, each of the quality appropriate to its intended use, purchased at the most favorable price.
    - Standards must be developed for the quality and quantity of food purchased, as well as the prices at which food is purchased.

4. Standard purchase specifications are useful to management, in part because they eliminate misunderstandings between buyers and purveyors, make competitive bidding possible, and facilitate checking food as it is received.

5. The purchasing routine for perishable foods should include determining amounts already on hand. Decisions also must be made as to total quantities needed. Once these quantities are determined, the difference between them is the correct amount to order.
    - Par stock is the quantity of any perishable item required to meet anticipated needs in a specific, upcoming period.

6. While nonperishable foods do not present rapid-deterioration problems, they do represent a considerable investment in stored material.
    - Fixing labels on shelves is one important step that should be taken in every storeroom.
    - Two basic methods to maintain inventories of nonperishables at appropriate levels are the periodic order and the perpetual inventory methods.
    - The periodic order method requires calculating the amount to order as:
      Amount required for the upcoming period – Amount presently on hand + Amount wanted on hand at the end of the period to last until the next delivery.
    - When using this method, managers must constantly review two quantities: normal usage and desired ending inventory, since many changes occur in usage from period to period.
    - In the perpetual inventory method, reorder quantities are calculated as:
      Par stock (maximum quantity that should be on hand) – Reorder point (number of units to which supply on hand should decrease before ordering) = Subtotal + Normal usage until delivery.

7. Foodservice operators depend on various suppliers, including wholesalers, local producers, manufacturers, packers, local farmers, retailers, and cooperative associations.

8. Purchasing stewards can obtain price quotations by phone, fax, mail, or fax modem; via the Internet; or from salespeople who continue to call on customers.

   - Ideally, the steward will obtain prices from several suppliers for each perishable item and will select the lowest price. The steward should also take into account delivery time and the reliability of dealers in providing foods meeting specifications.
   - For nonperishables, stewards often get extensive price lists from wholesale supply houses and use these to compare prices and make selections.

9. Purchasing personnel must be trained and monitored, and their work should be corrected if necessary.

10. Centralized purchasing systems are widely used by chains and, occasionally, established by small groups of independents with similar needs.

    - Some advantages of centralized purchasing include purchasing at lower prices (because of high volume), obtaining exact specifications, and fewer possibilities for dishonest purchasing.
    - Disadvantages include less buying freedom for the unit to purchase for its own particular needs and limits placed on the individual unit manager's freedom to change a menu.

11. Standing orders are arrangements made between purveyors and foodservice operators that result in regular delivery of goods without specific orders preceding each delivery.

12. Computers are being used increasingly in foodservice operations for more effective management of purchasing.

Chapter 4 Exercises

1. Match each definition, explanation, or term with the lettered corresponding term on the next page. Terms may be used more than once.

_____(1) Food items with a comparatively longer shelf life (L.O. 4.2)

_____(2) Number of units to which the supply on hand should decrease before additional orders are placed (L.O. 4.9)

_____(3) Includes columns for price quotations on each perishable product (L.O. 4.6)

_____(4) Inventory method requiring employees to maintain complete, accurate records (L.O. 4.7)

_____(5) Descriptions often based on grading standards established by the federal government (L.O. 4.5)

_____(6) Individual-unit orders are relayed to a central office that determines total requirements of all units and then purchases the total amount needed. (L.O. 4.14)

_____(7) Storage area in which nonperishables are kept (L.O. 4.2)

_____(8) Fresh fish and various kinds of lettuce (L.O. 4.2)

_____(9) Classroom instruction (L.O. 4.12)

_____(10) Groceries or staples (L.O. 4.2)

_____(11) Determined by storage space, limits on total value of inventory prescribed by management, desired frequency of ordering, usage, and vendors' minimum order requirements (L.O. 4.6)

_____(12) Foods with a comparatively short useful life (L.O. 4.2)

_____(13) Tool used for taking the daily inventory of perishables (L.O. 4.6)

_____(14) Delivery of goods without specific orders (L.O. 4.15)

_____(15) Maximum quantity of any item that should be on hand at any given time (L.O. 4.6)

_____(16) Used by virtually all purveyors to provide price quotations to customers and to receive orders (L.O. 4.11)

_____(17) Monitoring employee performance and comparing it to established standards and standard procedures (L.O. 4.1)

_____(18) Salt, sugar, flour, canned fruits, and spices (L.O. 4.2)

_____(19) List of all food items to be purchased (L.O. 4.5)

_____(20) Procedures for determining the appropriate amount of each item that should be purchased (L.O. 4.4)

_____(21) Label used to record quantities added to and taken from inventory (L.O. 4.7)

_____(22) Amount of nonperishables required for the upcoming period – Amount presently on hand + Amount wanted on hand at the end of the period to last until the next delivery = Amount to order (L.O. 4.7, 4.8)

_____(23) Amount of nonperishables that will be ordered each time the quantity of a particular item diminishes to the reorder point (L.O. 4.9)

_____(24) Basis for creating a list of foods required for day-to-day operations (L.O. 4.3)

_____(25) Most common way to maintain inventories of nonperishables, allowing for infrequent ordering (L.O. 4.7)

_____(26) Foods that should be purchased for immediate use (L.O. 4.2)

_____(27) Eliminates the need for detailed, verbal descriptions of a product each time it is ordered (L.O. 4.5)

_____(28) Simulation exercises (L.O. 4.12)

a. Menu
b. Quantity standards
c. Perishables
d. Par stock
e. Reorder quantity
f. Standard purchase specifications
g. Periodic order method
h. Training
i. Bin card

j. Step three in the control process
k. Steward's market quotation list
l. Storeroom
m. Standing orders
n. Nonperishables
o. Perpetual inventory method
p. Reorder point
q. Centralized purchasing
r. Fax machines

2. Write a standard purchase specification for one of the following:

Boneless chicken breast
Grouper
Granny Smith apples
Canned tomatoes
Frozen peas

_____

_____

_____

_____

L.O. 4.3–4.5

3. Name four general suppliers on whom foodservice operators depend.

- _____
- _____
- _____
- _____

L.O. 4.10

4. How might the purchasing steward's performance be monitored? Why is such monitoring necessary?

_____

_____

_____

L.O. 4.1, 4.13

5. Name two possible computer applications in foodservice purchasing.

- _____
- _____

L.O. 4.16

Chapter 4 Check-in

1. Food items that can be stored in the packages or containers in which they are received are called

   A. centralized foods.
   B. standard foods.
   C. nonperishable foods.
   D. perishable foods.

   L.O. 4.2

2. Which of the following help ensure that all foods purchased will be of the desired quality for their intended use?

   A. Quantity standards
   B. Purchase prices
   C. Standard purchase specifications
   D. Corrective actions

   L.O. 4.3, 4.5

3. The quantity of any item required to meet anticipated needs in a specific upcoming period is called

   A. Steward's market quotation list.
   B. periodic quantity.
   C. reorder point.
   D. par stock.

   L.O. 4.6

4. If Francesca's Italian Delight needs 60 cans of tomato paste for the upcoming period, 10 are on hand, and 5 are left at the end of the month, how many should be ordered?

   A. 55 cans
   B. 60 cans
   C. 65 cans
   D. 70 cans

   L.O. 4.8

5. When foodservice operators record quantities added to and taken from shelves on shelf labels, these labels are known as

   A. meat tags.
   B. bin cards.
   C. shelf markers.
   D. identifiers.

   L.O. 4.7

6. Par stock for kidney beans at Al's Eatery is 19 cans. If the reorder point is 10 cans and the reorder quantity for the period is 15 cans, what is the operation's normal usage until delivery?

   A. 4 cans
   B. 5 cans
   C. 6 cans
   D. 9 cans

   L.O. 4.9

7. The availability of sources of supply tends to be greatest

   A. during warm-weather months.
   B. through wholesalers.
   C. for suburban chains.
   D. in major metropolitan areas.

   L.O. 4.10

8. Which of the following is considered a "traditional" means for accessing price information?

   A. Direct computer links
   B. Fax machines
   C. Telephone quotations
   D. Modems

   L.O. 4.11

9. Any deviations from established purchasing standards require
    A. computerized applications.
    B. monetary incentives.
    C. training refreshers.
    D. corrective actions.

    L.O. 4.1, 4.12, 4.13

10. Desired quality can be more readily obtained with the use of
    A. centralized purchasing.
    B. standing orders.
    C. the perpetual inventory method.
    D. bin cards.

    L.O. 4.14

CHAPTER 5

FOOD RECEIVING CONTROL

Learning Objectives

5.1   Identify the primary purpose of receiving control.

5.2   List and explain three standards established to govern the receiving process.

5.3   List and explain the six steps of standard receiving procedure.

5.4   Describe the duties of a receiving clerk.

5.5   Outline the essential equipment and supplies needed for proper receiving.

5.6   List the categories of information contained on an invoice, and explain the invoice's function.

5.7   Explain the purposes of the invoice stamp.

5.8   List the categories of information contained in the receiving clerk's daily report, and explain the report's function.

5.9   Explain the difference between directs and stores, and provide examples of each.

5.10   Describe a meat tag, list the information found on it, and explain how it is used.

5.11   Explain why it is important to train receiving personnel.

5.12   Explain the need to monitor the performance of receiving personnel.

5.13   Describe one use of the computer in the receiving process.

Chapter 5 Study Outline

1. The primary purpose of receiving control is to verify that the quantity, quality, and price of each item delivered conforms to the order placed. It is, therefore, necessary to establish the following standards to govern the receiving process.
    *   The quantity of any item delivered should be the same as the quantity listed on the steward's market quotation list and the same as the quantity listed on the invoice.
    *   The quality of any item delivered should conform to the specification.
    *   The price should be the same as that circled on the steward's market quotation list.

2. The standard procedure for checking in deliveries includes the following steps:
   - Verify that the quantity, quality, and price for each item delivered conforms exactly to the order placed.
   - Sign the invoice or stamp with a rubber invoice stamp to acknowledge delivery quantities, quality, and prices.
   - List all invoices for foods delivered on a given day on the Receiving Clerk's Daily Report for that day. List items as directs or stores.
   - Fill out meat tags for appropriate items.
   - Forward completed paperwork to the proper person or persons.
   - Move food into storage as quickly as possible.
3. Training receiving employees is complex because they must be able to judge the quality of foods received.
4. To monitor receiving employees, managers can check deliveries after the receiving clerk has done so to compare results.
5. Corrective action might be necessary in order to improve employee performance.
6. Computers may be used by receiving clerks to track inventory and to compare items ordered with those received. They may also be used to track prices.

Chapter 5 Exercises

One challenge faced by managers who must train receiving personnel is the enormous amount of food knowledge required by these employees. Prepare a preliminary training program for receiving personnel at That Pizza Place. To do so, follow the steps and answer the questions below.

1. Explain the primary purpose and importance of receiving control.

   _____

   _____

   _____

L.O. 5.1

2. List the three standards necessary to govern the receiving process at That Pizza Place.
   - _____
   - _____
   - _____

L.O. 5.2

3. Provide an example on a separate sheet of paper of a typical invoice for the operation. Follow the form of the sample invoice in Figure 5.1 on text page 113.

L.O. 5.6

4. List the six components of the standard procedure detailed on text p.114, providing specific examples appropriate to That Pizza Place.

- _____
- _____
- _____
- _____
- _____
- _____

L.O. 5.3, 5.4

5. The receiving personnel at That Pizza Place must have specific supplies and forms, as well as various pieces of equipment, in order to verify the quantity, quality, and price of delivered items.

   a. Name three supplies or forms the receiving personnel will need.

   - _____
   - _____
   - _____

L.O. 5.5

   b. Why should receiving personnel at the operation use an invoice stamp?

   _____
   _____
   _____

L.O. 5.7

   c. On which form should receiving personnel copy data from each invoice to appropriate columns?

   _____

L.O. 5.8

d. Describe one use of the computer in the receiving process.

_____

_____

_____

L.O. 5.13

6. Drivers delivering food orders to That Pizza Place often do not have time to wait for verification to be completed. How should receiving personnel handle such situations?

_____

_____

_____

L.O. 5.3

7. Define and contrast directs and stores.

_____

_____

_____

L.O. 5.9

8. Why does That Pizza Place, like many other foodservice establishments, set up special controls for meat, poultry, fish, and shellfish? What is one of these controls, as discussed in the text?

_____

_____

_____

L.O. 5.10

9. Managers at That Pizza Place were surprised that Pete, the new receiving clerk, was unable to check the quality of delivered food items properly.

a. Should Pete be trained to check for quality?

_____

_____

_____

L.O. 5.11

b. How might managers monitor Pete's receiving performance?

_____

_____

_____

L.O. 5.12

Chapter 5 Check-in

1. The primary objective of receiving controls is to
   A. ensure that the foodservice operation makes a profit.
   B. verify that quantities, qualities, and prices of food delivered conform to orders placed.
   C. establish standards to govern the receiving process.
   D. acknowledge the work of receiving personnel.
   L.O. 5.1

2. The quality of a delivered item should conform to a foodservice establishment's
   A. standard purchase specification for that item.
   B. price projections.
   C. quantity standards.
   D. invoice.
   L.O. 5.2

3. Few foodservice establishments still use which of the following?
   A. Bin cards
   B. Hosts and hostesses
   C. Purchase journals
   D. Meat tags
   L.O. 5.3–5.5, 5.10

4. Which of the following requires extensive food knowledge and thorough investigation?
   A. Quantity verification
   B. Price verification
   C. Industry verification
   D. Quality verification
   L.O. 5.5

5. Verification of the date on which food was received can be provided by
   A. an invoice stamp.
   B. oral testimony.
   C. shelf labels.
   D. meat tags.
   L.O. 5.7

6. Which of the following will not diminish significantly in quality if not used immediately?
   A. Doughnuts
   B. Milk
   C. Fresh cauliflower
   D. Sugar
   L.O. 5.9

7. A summary of invoices for all foods received on a given day can be found on a(n)
   A. income statement.
   B. balance sheet.
   C. receiving clerk's daily report.
   D. computer-generated inventory spreadsheet.
   L.O. 5.8

8. Completed paperwork is forwarded to which of the following employees once all deliveries for the day are in?
   A. Steward
   B. Controller
   C. Owner/manager
   D. Chef
   L.O. 5.3

9. The big problem faced by those trying to train skilled receiving personnel is the
   A. trainer's ability to motivate employees.
   B. age of employees.
   C. training method employed.
   D. vast knowledge of foods these workers must have.
   L.O. 5.11

10. What common tool can be replaced when a computer is used to capture data on food items purchased and received
    A. Perpetual inventory cards
    B. Meat tags
    C. Bin cards
    D. Purchase requisitions
    L.O. 5.3

CHAPTER 6

FOOD STORING AND ISSUING CONTROL

Learning Objectives

6.1 List and explain three causes of unplanned costs that can develop while food is in storage.

6.2 List and explain five principal concerns that can be addressed by implementing standards for storing food.

6.3 Identify optimum storage temperatures for the five classifications of perishable foods.

6.4 Explain the importance of establishing standards for each of the following: storage temperatures for foods; storage containers for foods; shelving; cleanliness of storage facilities; and assigned locations for the storage of each particular food.

6.5 Explain the principle of stock rotation as applied to foodservice.

6.6 Distinguish between issuing procedures for directs and those for stores.

6.7 Describe the process used to price and extend a food requisition.

6.8 Describe five problem situations that can be avoided by properly training those who store and issue food.

6.9 Describe the primary technique for monitoring the performance of those who store and issue food.

6.10 Explain the difference between interunit and intraunit transfers, and give two examples of each.

6.11 Explain the significance of transfers in determining accurate food costs.

6.12 Explain the use of computers in establishing control over the storing, issuing, and transferring of foods.

Chapter 6 Study Outline

1. Three causes of unplanned costs that can develop while food is in storage are spoilage, waste, and theft.

2. To reduce or eliminate these costs, operators should establish standards for storing food that address the condition of facilities and equipment, the arrangement of foods, the location of facilities, the security of storage areas, and the dating and pricing of stored foods.

    *   The factors involved in maintaining proper internal conditions include temperature, storage containers, shelving, and cleanliness.
    *   The factors involved in maintaining appropriate internal arrangement of foods include keeping the most-used items readily available, fixing definite locations for each item, and rotating stock.
    *   Storage facilities should be located between receiving and preparation areas.
    *   Food should never be stored in a manner that permits theft, and storerooms should not be left unattended.
    *   Food items should be dated and priced as goods are put away on shelves.

3. The two elements in the issuing process are moving foods from storage facilities to food-preparation areas and keeping records associated with determining the cost of food issued.

4. Training for storing and issuing is not as difficult as training for purchasing, but it is just as important; storing and issuing personnel can be taught the proper methods and procedures by a qualified trainer.

5. To monitor storing and issuing performance, managers can inspect storage areas, observe how foods are being issued, and check that requisitions are properly priced and extended.

6. Foodservice operations must maintain records of the cost of food transferred.

    *   Intraunit transfers might be made between the bar and kitchen or between two or more kitchens.
    *   Interunit transfers often occur between units in a chain.

7. Computers can be used to code storage locations, eliminate the need for handwritten requisitions, and record cost information when food items are transferred.

Chapter 6 Exercises

1. Name three causes of unplanned costs that can develop while food is in storage.

    *   _____

    *   _____

    *   _____

L.O. 6.1

2. The manager at Sam's Deli has determined that a substantial portion of the establishment's costs over the last year have been unplanned. Most have been traced to improper storing and issuing at the operation. Indicate whether each of the following procedures at the deli is appropriate (A) or inappropriate (I).

_____a. Fresh fish is stored in stainless steel containers. (L.O. 6.2, 6.4)

_____b. Three keys to the storeroom have been issued to various employees. (L.O. 6.2)

_____c. Separate control procedures are in place for meat and liquor. (L.O. 6.2)

_____d. The following foods are stored at the temperatures indicated: fresh dairy products, fresh produce, and frozen foods: 35°F to 36°F; fresh meats: 40°F to 45°F; fresh fish: -10°F to 0°F. (L.O. 6.2, 6.3)

_____e. After stores have been issued, the storeroom clerk records on each requisition the cost of listed items and determines the total value of the food. (L.O. 6.7)

_____f. Spices are stored on solid steel shelving. (L.O. 6.2, 6.4)

_____g. Storage facilities are located adjacent to receiving areas, but far from food-preparation areas. (L.O. 6.2)

_____h. All items are priced as goods are put away. (L.O. 6.2)

_____i. The most frequently used items are kept farthest from the storage facility entrance to decrease the possibilities for theft. (L.O. 6.2)

_____j. The unit cost of each staple is marked on each container as it is stored. (Note: Sam's Deli uses a complete computer system.) (L.O. 6.7)

_____k. Storerooms are swept and cleaned on a daily basis. (L.O. 6.2, 6.4)

_____l. Older quantities of any item are used after any new deliveries have been depleted. (L.O. 6.2, 6.5)

3. Explain the differences in issuing procedure for directs and stores.

_____

_____

_____

_____

_____

L.O. 6.6

4. Name five problem situations that can be avoided by properly training employees who store and issue food.

    - _____
    - _____
    - _____
    - _____
    - _____

L.O. 6.8

5. Indicate whether each of the following statements is true (T) or false (F).

    _____a. Food and beverage transfers between departments of a food and beverage operation are called interunit transfers. (L.O. 6.10)

    _____b. The central technique for monitoring the performance of employees who store and issue food is to observe the results of their work. (L.O. 6.9)

    _____c. Transfers of food and beverage between units in a chain are called intraunit transfers. (L.O. 6.10)

    _____d. The use of computer applications in storing and issuing makes it possible for a foodservice establishment to eliminate handwritten requisitions entirely. (L.O. 6.12)

    _____e. The food controller uses records of transfers made to adjust food-cost figures to achieve greater accuracy. (L.O. 6.10)

Chapter 6 Check-in

1. The foodservice industry's term for theft, which is often associated with the storage and issuing functions, is

   A. spoilage.
   B. waste.
   C. pilferage.
   D. stealing.

   L.O. 6.1

2. Which of the following food items should be stored at 34°F to 36°F degrees?

   A. Frozen peas
   B. Fresh leg of lamb
   C. Fresh flounder
   D. Rye bread

   L.O. 6.2–6.4

3. Cooked foods and opened canned foods should be stored in

   A. stainless steel containers.
   B. shaved ice.
   C. their original containers.
   D. foil wrappers.

   L.O. 6.4

4. Which of the following reduces the possibilities for spoilage?

   A. Locating most-used food items closest to the storeroom entrance
   B. Locating storage facilities between receiving areas and preparation areas, preferably close to both
   C. Sealing dry-storage areas
   D. FIFO

   L.O. 6.2, 6.5

5. Which of the following tends to be artificially high on days when all directs received have not been consumed?

   A. Daily cost of food
   B. Transfer cost
   C. Staple consumption
   D. Customer satisfaction

   L.O. 6.6

6. If 30 pounds of sugar are purchased at a unit cost of $0.50, which extended cost should appear on the requisition?

   A. $1.50
   B. $15.00
   C. $15.50
   D. $150.00

   L.O. 6.7

7. By training storing and issuing personnel, which of the following potential problems can a restaurant avoid?

   A. Discipline issues arising from rebellious employees
   B. Each food item being stored in a single location
   C. Value of issues being readily identifiable
   D. Old deliveries being stored in front of new ones

   L.O. 6.8

8. The primary technique for monitoring the work of those who store and issue food is to
   A. install close-circuit television cameras.
   B. employ undercover inspectors.
   C. impose stringent reporting requirements.
   D. observe the results of their performance.
   L.O. 6.9

9. Which of the following is an example of an interunit transfer?
   A. One unit of a chain produces and distributes baked goods to other units.
   B. A food department purchases wine from a beverage department to create a sauce.
   C. The vice president of a company's U.S. division moves to another division in Switzerland.
   D. Many generations of one family work for the same foodservice operation.
   L.O. 6.10

10. A printer installed in a storeroom can print a chef's "requisition" and make it instantly available to those who fill it through the use of a(n)
    A. e-mail address.
    B. local area network.
    C. Internet connection.
    D. modem.
    L.O. 6.12

CHAPTER 7

Learning Objectives

7.1 Explain the importance of standard portion sizes, standard recipes, and standard portion costs to foodservice operations.

7.2 Identify four methods for determining standard portion costs, and describe the type of food product for which each is used.

7.3 Calculate standard portion costs using four different methods.

7.4 Use cost factors derived from butcher tests and cooking loss tests to recalculate portion costs as market prices change.

7.5 Use yield factors derived from butcher tests and cooking loss tests to determine correct purchase quantities.

7.6 Describe the levels of knowledge and skill needed by food production employees, and explain the effect of these on the approaches management takes to training food production workers.

7.7 Describe several ways computers are used in controlling production.

Chapter 7 Study Outline

1. Standards and standard procedures necessary in food production include standard portion size, standard recipe, and standard portion cost.
   - Every item on a menu can be quantified by weight, volume, or count.
   - Standard recipes ensure that the quality of any item will be the same each time the item is produced.
2. Standard portion cost can be derived by formula, recipe detail and cost cards, butcher tests, or cooking loss tests.
   - For many menu items, the standard portion cost can be determined with the following formula: Purchase price per unit ÷ Number of portions per unit = Standard portion cost.

- For menu items produced from standard recipes, it is possible to determine the standard cost of one portion by costing out the recipe on a recipe detail and cost card.
- The butcher test and cooking loss test are used to calculate costs of menu items that need processing. Generally, the butcher test is used for those items portioned before cooking, while the cooking loss test is used for those items portioned after cooking.
- In the butcher test, a piece of meat is trimmed and the amount of usable meat is turned into a percentage as follows:

  Weight of usable meat ÷ Purchased weight = Percentage usable meat (Yield percentage, or Yield factor).
- To determine the cost per usable pound, use the following formula:

  Total value of usable meat ÷ Weight of usable meat = Cost per usable pound.
- Divide the cost per usable pound by 16 to get the cost per usable ounce. The portion cost is calculated by multiplying the portion size in ounces by the cost of each usable ounce:

  Portion size × Cost per usable ounce = Portion cost.
- The following formula helps to determine new portion costs when the dealer's price changes:

  Cost factor per pound × Portion size (expressed as a decimal) × Dealer price per pound. = Portion cost.
- In a cooking loss test, the cost of each usable pound is calculated exactly as in the butcher test, but the number of usable pounds is weighed after the meat is cooked.

3. Once determined, yield percentages can be used in a number of quantity calculations. The general formula is:

   Number of portions × Portion size (as a decimal) ÷ Yield percentage = Quantity.

4. Having established standards and standard procedures to control production, the next logical step is to train staff members to follow standards.

- Management needs to determine the particular knowledge and skill levels required by employees in specific jobs.
- Regardless of the level of knowledge and skill an employee has, some training is needed for all production workers in foodservice if standards and standard procedures established to control production are to be met.

5. To monitor production performance, managers can observe production in progress, taste foods, weigh uncooked portions of some entree items, and observe plated foods as they are about to be served.

- Indirect methods include checking on customers' reactions to products and investigating complaints.

6. Computers can be used for recipe costing.

Chapter 7 Exercises

1. Name three consequences of serving portions of the same menu item in varying sizes.

    *   _____

    *   _____

    *   _____

L.O. 7.1

2. The manager at Claire's Cafe wants to calculate the standard portion cost for four menu items. Each item requires use of a different method. Find the standard portion cost for each using the information provided.

    a. Peach slices are served with pancakes, pie, and cottage cheese, with four slices as the standard portion. Claire's receives the peaches canned, in heavy syrup, with 30 slices per can. The cans are ordered by the dozen, with each dozen costing $15.50. Find the standard portion cost.

    _____

    _____

L.O. 7.2, 7.3

b. Claire's serves a variety of burgers. The following recipe is for the restaurant's oat-bran hamburger:

2 pounds. ground beef
1/2 cup oat-bran cereal
2 large, minced garlic cloves
1/2 cup finely chopped onions
1/4 cup finely chopped green pepper
1 1/2 teaspoons salt
Mix all ingredients and form into eight patties. Cook for twenty minutes at 375°F, flipping burgers after the first ten minutes.

Cost information is as follows:

Item	Cost
Ground beef	$2.19 per pound
Oat-bran cereal	$4.00 per box (each box contains 10 cups)
Garlic cloves	$0.10 each
Onions	$0.40 each (1 onion = 1 cup chopped)
Green peppers	$0.40 each (1 green pepper = 1 cup chopped)
Salt	$0.05 (for this recipe)

Create a recipe detail and cost card on a separate sheet of paper for Claire's oat-bran hamburger. (Refer to Figure 7.2 on text page 160 if necessary.) Calculate the standard portion cost.

L.O. 7.2, 7.3

c. On the premium side, Claire's offers filet mignon (from U.S. choice beef tenderloin).
    (1) Given the following information, complete a butcher test card on a separate sheet of paper for this menu item. (Refer to Figure 7.3 if necessary.)

Weight of beef tenderloin purchased: 10 pounds
Price per lb.: $5.16
Portion size: 8 ounces
Breakdown—fat: 4 pounds, 2 ounces; value of fat per pound: $0.12; usable meat: 4 pounds, 8 ounces

    (2) If the dealer price per pound of beef tenderloin increases to $5.98 per pound, what is the new portion cost?

L.O. 7.4

(3) If Claire's wants to provide eight-ounce portions of filet mignon to 40 people, how much beef tenderloin should be purchased? (Use the yield percentage you calculated in Part a of this question.)

L.O. 7.5

d. Claire's leg of lamb is the best in town. Complete a cooking loss test card on a separate sheet of paper for the lamb, which is cooked for one hour and five minutes at 375°F. (Refer to Figure 7.4 on text page 168 if necessary.)

Price per lb.: $6.20
Original weight: 7 pounds
Trimmed weight: 5 pounds, 12 ounces
Cooked weight: 5 pounds, 1 ounces
Bones and trim: 1 pound
Portion size: 4 ounces

3. Contrast the levels of knowledge and skill needed by food production employees at quick-service establishments and those at a fine hotel restaurant.

L.O. 7.6

4. Name one way in which computers can be used in controlling food production.

L.O. 7.7

Chapter 7 Check-in

1. The quantity of any item to be served each time that item is ordered is referred to as

    A. standard portion size.
    B. standard recipe.
    C. standard portion cost.
    D. identity item.

L.O. 7.1

2. Which of the following is commonly used to measure portions of soup?

    A. Weight
    B. Volume
    C. Count
    D. Density

L.O. 7.1

3. Which of the following helps ensure that the quality of any menu item will be the same each time it is produced?

    A. Low employee turnover
    B. Standard recipe
    C. Cooking loss test
    D. Yield factor
    L.O. 7.1

4. If two eggs are the standard portion at Mickey's Breakfast Place, what is the standard cost of the portion of a 40-dozen case of eggs that costs $50.50?

    A. $0.19
    B. $0.21
    C. $0.30
    D. $0.32
    L.O. 7.2, 7.3

5. It is not worthwhile to calculate the actual value of which of the following?

    A. Inexpensive ingredients used in small portions
    B. Meat, poultry, and seafood
    C. Dairy products
    D. Baked goods
    L.O. 7.3

6. If 8 ounces of a 12-pound piece of meat is lost in cutting, what is the ratio of loss to total weight?

    A. 0.042%
    B. 0.42%
    C. 4.2%
    D. 42.0%
    L.O. 7.3

7. If the dealer price for a 12-ounce steak has gone up to $6.77 per pound and the cost factor per pound is 2.0455, what is the portion cost?

    A. $4.56
    B. $9.16
    C. $10.39
    D. $15.95
    L.O. 7.4

8. If the yield percentage for eight-ounce portions of leg of lamb to be served to 48 people is 46.5%, how much lamb should be purchased?

    A. 18 pounds
    B. 33 pounds
    C. 42 pounds
    D. 67 pounds
    L.O. 7.5

9. An important aspect of training is often to ensure that each new production worker has access to

    A. wage increase criteria.
    B. the establishment's sexual harassment policy.
    C. security procedures.
    D. a list of standard portion sizes.
    L.O. 7.6

10. Many foodservice establishments use computer programs for which production function?

    A. Accounting
    B. Butcher testing
    C. Yield percentage determination
    D. Recipe costing
    L.O. 7.7

CHAPTER 8

Learning Objectives

8.1   Define the standard for controlling production volume, and explain its importance.

8.2   List and describe three standard procedures that enable managers to gain control over production volume.

8.3   Define *sales history* and describe two methods for gathering the data from which a sales history is developed.

8.4   List three basic approaches to arranging data in a sales history.

8.5   Define *popularity index*.

8.6   Calculate a popularity index for menu items.

8.7   Use a popularity index to forecast portion sales.

8.8   Describe the production sheet and calculate needed production for menu items.

8.9   Describe a void sheet and explain its use.

8.10   Complete a portion inventory and reconciliation.

8.11   Describe a procedure used for controlling high-cost, preportioned entrees.

8.12   Describe the use of computers in forecasting sales and controlling production quantities.

Chapter 8 Study Outline

1. The standard for controlling production volume is to determine and produce the number of portions likely to be sold on any given day.

2. To control production volume, it is necessary to establish appropriate standard procedures. These include maintaining sales history, either manually or electronically, forecasting portion sales, and determining production quantities.

   - A sales history is a written record of the number of portions of each menu item sold every time that item appeared on the menu.
   - Managers should include in the sales history any information about conditions (such as weather conditions) and events (such as holidays) that affected sales and that should be considered in forecasting sales volume for a future period.

3. Sales history information can be used to determine popularity index:
   Portion sales for Item A ÷ Total portion sales for all menu items = Popularity index for Item A.

   - The popularity index can be useful in determining whether to continue offering a certain item on the menu.

4. A production sheet is used to determine production quantities.

   - The sheet lists the names and quantities of all menu items to be prepared for a given date and then translates management's portion-sales forecasts into production targets.

5. Management must take great care to train staff to record complete and accurate production data.

   - Training personnel for forecasting requires selecting those with experience and judgment.

6. To monitor performance, managers can compare the sales forecast to actual sales in order to make judgments about the accuracy of the forecast. They can compare production records to sales records in order to determine the extent to which kitchen production matched the production sheet.

   - The void sheet records information about returned portions.
   - The portion inventory and reconciliation sheet allows managers to determine how closely the chef has followed quantity-production standards.
   - The number of preportioned entrées the steward issues should be equal to the number of sales forecasted for each item.

7. Computers can be helpful in developing records for sales histories, for maintaining sales history, and for forecasting.

Chapter 8 Exercises

Many records, forms, and control sheets are helpful in applying the control process to the quantity-production phase of foodservice operations. For each of the following forms:

a. Explain its purpose.
b. Describe in detail how it is used.
c. Answer any other questions posed about it.

1. Portion sales breakdown

_____

_____

_____

L.O. 8.2, 8.3

2. Sales history

_____

_____

_____

    a. In what three ways can sales data be arranged in a sales history?

_____

_____

L.O. 8.2, 8.3, 8.4

3. Popularity index

_____

_____

_____

    a. What is the definition of *popularity index*?

_____

_____

b. Given the following information, determine the popularity index for each menu item.

Menu Item	Portions sold on Monday	Popularity Index
A	85	
B	23	
C	77	
D	93	

c. If item C usually represents 30% of total sales on Monday evenings, forecast the portion sales for item C for next Monday.

_____

_____

L.O. 8.5–8.7

4. Production sheet

_____

_____

_____

L.O. 8.8

5. Void sheet

_____

_____

_____

a. Name one reason a menu item may be rejected and returned.

_____

_____

_____

L.O. 8.9

6. Portion inventory and reconciliation

_____

_____

_____

L.O. 8.10

7. Control sheet for preportioned entrées

_____

_____

_____

L.O. 8.11

Chapter 8 Check-in

1. The standard for controlling production volume is to determine and produce, for any menu item, the number of portions that, on any given day, is likely to be

    A. sold.
    B. rejected by customers.
    C. forecasted.
    D. maintained.

    L.O. 8.1

2. A summary of portion sales is known as the

    A. sales history.
    B. sales forecast.
    C. popularity index.
    D. void sheet.

    L.O. 8.2, 8.3

3. Portion sales records are likely to be arranged by

    A. day of the week.
    B. server.
    C. sales price.
    D. historical record.

    L.O. 8.4

4. The ratio of portion sales for a given menu item to total portion sales for all menu items is known as

    A. cost-benefit ratio.
    B. portion statement.
    C. popularity index.
    D. sales history.

    L.O. 8.5

5. Of the 246 items sold last Tuesday night at Nathan's Steak House, 55 portions were T-bone steak. What is the popularity index for this menu item?

   A. 22.4%
   B. 24.8%
   C. 26.0%
   D. 30.3%

   L.O. 8.6

6. If T-bone steak usually represents 40% of total sales at Nathan's Steak House on Tuesday evenings, forecast the portion sales for the menu item for next Tuesday, based on the information in Question 5.

   A. 86
   B. 90
   C. 98
   D. 104

   L.O. 8.7

7. Which of the following control tools lists the names and quantities of all menu items to be prepared for a given date?

   A. Void sheet
   B. Production sheet
   C. Sales forecast
   D. Budget

   L.O. 8.8

8. A void sheet reflecting returns that are consistently high and evenly distributed among job classifications can be indicative of

   A. inattention to customer orders by particular servers.
   B. inadequate employee performance.
   C. inflation.
   D. general understaffing.

   L.O. 8.9

9. The number of preportioned entrées that a steward issues should be equal to the number of sales

   A. returned.
   B. recorded.
   C. forecasted.
   D. desired.

   L.O. 8.11

10. Developing sales history data has become simpler and faster than in the past with the use of

    A. electronic sales terminals.
    B. portion inventory and reconciliation.
    C. advanced forecasting techniques.
    D. trend analysis.

    L.O. 8.12

CHAPTER 9

MONITORING FOODSERVICE OPERATIONS I: MONTHLY INVENTORY AND MONTHLY FOOD COST

Learning Objectives

9.1   Explain the importance of monitoring a foodservice operation to assess monthly performance.

9.2   Describe the procedure for taking physical inventory at the end of the month.

9.3   List and explain five ways to assign unit costs to a food inventory.

9.4   Calculate cost of food consumed.

9.5   Explain the effect on cost of each of five acceptable methods of assigning unit costs to a closing inventory.

9.6   Make adjustments to cost of food consumed in order to determine cost of food sold.

9.7   Distinguish between the terms *opening* (or *beginning*) *inventory* and *closing* (or *ending*) *inventory*.

9.8   Explain the relationship between the monthly calculation of cost of food sold and the monthly income statement.

9.9   Prepare a simple monthly food cost report.

9.10 Calculate cost of food consumed, cost of food sold, food cost percent, and food cost per dollar sale.

9.11 Explain the possible shortcomings of a system in which judgments about operations are made exclusively on the basis of monthly food cost and food cost percent.

9.12 Explain how computers are used to value inventories and to verify employee adherence to standard procedures for issuing foods from inventory.

Chapter 9 Study Outline

1. There are five accepted methods for assigning values to units of the products in inventory:
   - Actual purchase price method
   - First-in, first out (FIFO) method (latest prices)
   - Weighted average purchase price method
   - Latest purchase price method
   - Last-in, first out method (earliest prices)

2. The cost of food sold for any month is determined by means of the following formula:

	Opening inventory
+	Purchases
=	Total available
−	Closing inventory
=	Cost of food

3. The monthly determination of cost of food consumed is determined as follows, taking adjustments into account:

	Opening inventory
+	Purchases
=	Total available for sale
−	Closing inventory
=	Cost of food issued
+	Cooking liquor
+	Transfer from other units
−	Food to bar (directs)
−	Transfers to other units
−	Grease sales
−	Steward sales
−	Gratis to bar
−	Promotion expense
=	Cost of food consumed

4. To reach an accurate figure for cost of food sold, subtract the cost of employee meals from cost of food consumed:

	Cost of food consumed
−	Cost of employee meals
=	Cost of food sold

   - Employee meals can be determined by cost of separate issues, prescribed amount per meal per employee, prescribed amount per period, or sales value multiplied by cost percent.

5. Once food cost is known, food cost percent can be calculated by using the following formula:

   Cost ÷ Sales = Cost percent.

6. Once food cost percent and cost of food sold have been calculated, they are usually reported to management.
   - Reports should be based on management's need for specific information.
   - For many foodservice managers, monthly reports are not truly useful for monitoring operations because they fail to meet two import criteria: frequency and timeliness.
   - Many managers prefer weekly or daily reports so they can identify problems and immediately take correction action.
7. Inventory turnover can be calculated using the following formulas:
   - Total inventory = Opening inventory + Closing inventory
   - Total inventory ÷ 2= Average inventory
   - Food cost ÷ Average inventory = Inventory turnover
8. Computers can be used to calculate the value of a closing inventory and to prepare management reports.

Chapter 9 Exercises

1. How many people are required to take physical inventory in a foodservice operation and what are their roles?

   _____

   _____

   _____

L.O. 9.2

2. Records for the month indicate the following information regarding 48-ounce cans of tomato juice in stores inventory at Jim's Place.

Opening inventory on the 1st of the month	7 cans @ $1.01 = $7.07
Purchased on the 7th of the month	16 cans @ $0.99 = $15.84
Purchased on the 15th of the month	14 cans @ $1.15 = $16.10
Purchased on the 26th of the month	3 cans @ $1.07 = $3.21

   A physical inventory on the last day of the month shows the following:

Opening inventory	7 cans
+ Purchases during the month	33 cans
= Total available	40 cans
– Closing inventory	8 cans
= Units consumed	32 cans

a. Assign values to the units in closing inventory using the following methods:
   (1) Actual purchase price, if three cans were purchased on the 7th, one can on the 15th, and four cans on the 26th

   _____

   (2) First-in, first-out

   _____

   (3) Weighted average purchase price

   _____

   (4) Latest purchase price

   _____

   (5) Last-in, first-out

   _____

L.O. 9.3, 9.5

b. What is the percentage difference between the highest value and the lowest value for these eight cans of tomato juice? Why is this difference significant?

   _____

   _____

   _____

L.O. 9.5

51

3. Given the following total, month-end inventory information for Jim's Place, determine cost of food consumed, cost of food sold, and food cost percent. Food sales for the month were $16,500.

Opening inventory	$2,500.00
Transfers from other units	$200.00
Grease sales	$30.00
Gratis to bar	$85.00
Promotion	$25.00
Purchases	$7,000.00
Steward sales	$10.00
Cooking liquor	$150.00
Transfers to other units	$400.00
Food to bar	$70.00
Closing inventory	$4,000.00
25 employee lunches at $2.00 each	$50.00
27 employee dinners at $4.00 each	$108.00

_____Cost of food consumed

_____Cost of food sold

_____Food cost percent

L.O. 9.4, 9.6, 9.7, 9.10

4. Managers at Jim's Place have decided that monthly food cost information is not sufficient for monitoring the operation. Why did they make this decision?

_____

_____

_____

L.O. 9.11

5. Based on the information provided above what was Jim's inventory turnover for the month? How does it compare to the average inventory turnover for most foodservice operations?

_____

_____

_____

L.O. 9.11

6. How can a foodservice establishment like Jim's Place use computers to monitor inventory and monthly food cost?

_____

_____

_____

L.O. 9.12

Chapter 9 Check-in

1. Basic monthly food cost calculations can provide some reasonable estimate of
   A. the quantity standards in place in a foodservice operation.
   B. sales for the most current period.
   C. standard portion cost.
   D. overall financial health of a foodservice establishment through the end of the most recent month.
   L.O. 9.1

2. Providing a list of goods on hand so that the value of the goods can be determined and recorded is the purpose of
   A. calculating the cost of food consumed.
   B. taking physical inventory.
   C. determining the value of transfers.
   D. training food-production employees.
   L.O. 9.2

3. Which of the following automatically becomes the opening inventory for the next period?
   A. Beginning inventory for the period
   B. Cost of food consumed for the period
   C. Food cost percent for the period
   D. Closing inventory for the period
   L.O. 9.7

4. Multiplying the number of units in the opening inventory and in each subsequent purchase by their specific purchase price, adding these values, and then dividing the total by the total number of units determines which of the following?
   A. Latest purchase price
   B. Weighted average purchase price
   C. FIFO price
   D. LIFO price
   L.O. 9.3

5. Which method is most commonly used to assign unit costs to a closing inventory?
   A. FIFO method
   B. LIFO method
   C. Latest purchase price method
   D. Actual purchase price method
   L.O. 9.3, 9.5

6. Saying that food cost percent is 31.8% is the same as saying that

    A. the contribution margin is .318.
    B. monthly food cost information is insufficient.
    C. the cost of food has been $0.682 per dollar sale.
    D. the cost of food has been $0.318 per dollar sale.

    L.O. 9.10

7. Raw fat kept under refrigeration until disposal is known as

    A. steward grease.
    B. gratis to bar.
    C. grease sales.
    D. cooking oil.

    L.O. 9.4

8. If the cost of food consumed is $45,900 and the cost of food sold is $44,810, what is the cost of employees' meals?

    A. $1,090
    B. $5,500
    C. $10,090
    D. $89,710

    L.O. 9.6

9. Reports to management should always be based on

    A. monthly cost figures.
    B. management's need for specific information.
    C. categories indicated on report forms.
    D. the best possible figures.

    L.O. 9.9

10. Which of the following figures provide management with the most realistically accurate and helpful cost information?

    A. Daily cost figures
    B. Weekly cost figures
    C. Monthly cost figures
    D. Annual cost figures

    L.O. 9.11

CHAPTER 10

Learning Objectives

10.1   Calculate food cost for any one day and for all the days to date in a period.

10.2   Calculate food cost percent for any one day and for all the days to date in a period.

10.3   Prepare a daily report of food sales, food cost, and food cost percent.

10.4   Determine book inventory value.

10.5   Explain the difference between book inventory and actual inventory.

10.6   Identify various causes for differences between book inventory value and actual inventory value.

10.7   Explain how computers can be used for generating daily food cost reports.

Chapter 10 Study Outline

1. Since all foods can be categorized as either directs or stores in food control, the total costs for these two are the basic components of the daily food cost.

2. The daily cost of food can be determined in the following way:

	Cost of directs (from the receiving clerk's daily report)
+	Cost of stores (from requisitions and, sometimes, meat tags)
+	Adjustments that increase daily cost (transfers from bar to kitchen, transfers from other units)
−	Adjustments that decrease daily cost (transfers from the kitchen to the bar, gratis to bar, steward sales, grease sales, promotion expense)
=	Cost of food consumed
−	Cost of employee meals
=	Daily cost of food sold

3. After determining daily food cost, the next step is to obtain a daily sales figure, usually from accounting records. When both food cost and food sales figures are known, a daily food cost percent can be determined.

4. To help overcome the problem of artificially high food cost percent one day and low food cost percent the next, many foodservice operations also calculate food cost percent to date by dividing cost to date by sales to date.

5. A basic daily report will include daily figures for food cost, food sales, and food cost percent, and then compare these figures to those for a similar period.

- In addition, it will include cumulative figures for the period for food cost, food sales, and food cost percent.
- When the information is presented in this way, it is easier to monitor operations—to complete operating results for similar periods, to make judgments about the effectiveness of current operations, and to take corrective action if necessary.

6. Some foodservice operators determine book inventory—the value of what the closing inventory should be—based on records indicating purchases and issues.

- Book inventory value is usually compared to actual inventory value.
- Book inventory value is determined as follows:

$$
\begin{array}{ll}
& \text{Opening inventory} \\
+ & \text{Purchases (total stores purchased for the period, as listed on receiving reports)} \\
\underline{-} & \underline{\text{Issues (as listed on requisitions)}} \\
= & \text{Closing book value of the stores inventory}
\end{array}
$$

- Depending on the size of an operation and the volume involved, discrepancies of some small percentage between book inventory and physical inventory can often be attributed to acceptable causes and are of no further concern, except that employees should be made aware of any errors made. When discrepancies are more substantial, however, management has a responsibility to investigate, identify causes, and take corrective action.

7. Computers can be used to prepare frequent and timely reports that provide quick and easy access to the information managers require to make operating decisions.

Chapter 10 Exercises

1. Why do foodservice operations use daily, rather than weekly or monthly, food cost calculations?

_____

_____

_____

L.O. 10.1

2. How are directs and stores charged to food cost?

_____

_____

_____

L.O. 10.1, 10.2

3. How is daily food cost determined?

_____

_____

_____

L.O. 10.1, 10.2

4. Why might food cost percent be artificially high one day and low the next? How can this problem be corrected?

_____

_____

_____

L.O. 10.2

5. On the following page is information for Maddy's Pub for the week of January 17 through 22.
    a. Complete the daily cumulative cost record shown on the following page for the week of 1/17 through 1/22.

L.O. 10.1, 10.2

    b. If food sales for the previous week were $9,520.00, and food cost was $2,910.00, prepare a simple food cost report on a separate sheet of papershowing cost and sales information for 1/17, the current week, and the previous week. Use Figure 10.4 on text page 239 as a guide.

L.O. 10.3

6. What is book inventory? How is it different from actual inventory?

_____

_____

_____

L.O. 10.5

Exercise 5

Maddy's Pub, January 17-22

Date	Directs	Meat	Stores	Adjustments		Total Cost		Total Sales		Food Cost %	
				Beverage to Food	Food to Beverage	Today	To Date	Today	To Date	Today	To Date
1/17	$300	$200	$150	$25	-0-			$2,000			
1/18	$175	$150	$150	-0-	$30			$1,500			
1/19	$200	$250	$120	-0-	$20			$1,600			
1/20	$100	$90	$100	-0-	-0-			$1,000			
1/21	$425	$300	$100	$50	-0-			$3,000			
1/22	$75	$110	$150	-0-	-0-			$900			

7. Find the book inventory value for DeeDee's Diner for each of the three days below.

Date	Purchases	Issues	Inventory balance
31-May			$4,850.00
1-June	$300.00	$175.00	
2-June	$200.00	$240.00	
3-June	$400.00	$100.00	

L.O. 10.4

8. What are some of the reasons—acceptable and unacceptable—that book inventory value never equals the physical inventory value taken at the end of the month?

_____

_____

_____

_____

L.O. 10.6

9. If numerical codes were assigned to food items at Rebecca's Seafood Emporium to maintain computerized purchase and inventory records, as discussed in the text, which would provide a more detailed report, four-digit codes or five-digit codes? Why?

_____

_____

_____

L.O. 10.7

Chapter 10 Check-in

1. What are the two basic components of the daily food cost?

   A. Directs and stores
   B. Fixed cost and variable cost
   C. Contribution rate and contribution margin
   D. Food cost and beverage cost

   L.O. 10.1

2. A food controller can determine the total of directs received on a particular day from

   A. requisitions.
   B. invoices.
   C. the receiving clerk's daily report.
   D. the menu.

   L.O. 10.1

3. If the daily cost of food sold at Reggie's Hot Dog Stand is $445.00 on June 28 and food sales were $1,205.00 for the day, what is the establishment's food cost percent for June 28?

   A. 27.4%
   B. 32.0%
   C. 36.9%
   D. 38.2%

   L.O. 10.2

4. The figure that takes into account all food costs and all food sales for all days so far in the period is known as

   A. total food cost percent.
   B. grand food cost.
   C. 100% of food cost.
   D. food cost percent to date.

   L.O. 10.2

5. Which of the following information on food cost reports helps managers make judgments about the effectiveness of current operations?

   A. Operating results for similar periods
   B. Daily figures
   C. Cumulative totals
   D. Requisition order numbers

   L.O. 10.3

6. What is the likely cause of increasing ratios between direct costs and sales when both customer demand and market conditions remain constant?

   A. Changes in the sales mix
   B. Problems in kitchen operations
   C. Employee turnover
   D. Morale issues

   L.O. 10.3

7. The value of all items counted in inventory is called

   A. book inventory.
   B. closing inventory.
   C. real inventory.
   D. physical inventory.

   L.O. 10.5

8. If purchases for the month of July for the Mandarin House were $4,000, opening inventory was $6,000, and issues were $3,000, what was the establishment's closing book value of the stores inventory?

   A. $5,000
   B. $7,000
   C. $9,000
   D. $11,000

   L.O. 10.4

9. Which of the following is an acceptable reason for the difference in values of book inventory and actual closing inventory?
    A. Theft of food
    B. Allowing meat to age to the extent it becomes unusable
    C. Mismarking of actual purchase prices on items when that method is used
    D. Issuing stores without requisitions

L.O. 10.6

10. Which of the following can ensure that sales data are readily available?
    A. Sales terminals
    B. Computer software
    C. Assignment of numerical codes to food items
    D. The Internet

L.O. 10.7

CHAPTER 11

MONITORING FOODSERVICE OPERATIONS III: ACTUAL VS. STANDARD FOOD COSTS

Learning Objectives

11.1   Define *standard cost* and explain how it is calculated.

11.2   Describe how to use a menu pre-cost and abstract form.

11.3   List three ways an undesirable forecasted food cost percent could be changed.

11.4   Define potential savings and list several conditions that impact it.

11.5   Distinguish between daily and periodic calculation of standard cost and potential savings.

11.6   Explain the role of the computer in determining potential savings.

Chapter 11 Study Outline

1. Standard cost is the agreed-upon cost of goods or services used to measure other costs. Actual costs can be compared to standard costs, and any difference between them will be a useful measure of the extent to which the standards and standard procedures are being followed.

2. There are two methods for comparing actual and standard costs.
    *   The first requires daily calculation of standard costs and actual costs for the day and for all the days thus far in the operating period—the week or the month. Daily reports are prepared to compare actual and standard costs to date. The last of these in a given period is a final summary report for the period.
    *   The second method does not require daily calculation, relying instead on periodic determination of standard costs from records or actual portion sales in the period.

3. The menu pre-cost and abstract form is helpful in comparing actual costs to standard costs using either method.

- The section on the left of the form is based on a sales forecast prepared some time before a day or meal. The section on the right (the abstract) is completed later, after the day or meal for which the forecast was prepared.
- A standard cost percent based on actual portions sold is determined by dividing total standard costs by total sales.
- By comparing the cost percent determined on each side of the form, one can see how accurate the forecast was and the number of inefficiencies in day-to-day operations, such as poor forecasting, overproduction, failure to follow standard recipes, and overpurchasing.
- It is useful to develop abstracts of standard costs and sales over a period of some days or weeks and then summarize the results. Taken together, the days or weeks can be considered a test period, with the results offering a good indication of an acceptable level for food cost percent over time.

4. An undesirable forecasted food cost percent can be altered by changing sales prices, changing standard portion costs, or adding or eliminating menu items.

5. Potential savings (the difference between actual costs and standard costs) can be recorded as dollars, as percentages of sales, or as both.

- Reasons for differences between standard and actual costs could include overpurchasing, overproduction, pilferage, spoilage, improper portioning, and failure to follow standard recipes.
- Reducing potential savings means reducing waste and excessive cost. It will never be possible to completely eliminate discrepancies between actual and standard costs. To the extent that savings can be achieved without incurring other costs, profits will be increased.

6. In establishments where daily calculations of standard costs and potential savings are impractical or impossible, it is often possible to do periodic comparisons.

- The periodic method assumes that standards and standard procedures have been established, that sales histories are maintained, and that standard portion costs are known.
- Under these circumstances, one can calculate standard cost for a test period and compare that figure to actual cost for the same period to determine the extent of potential savings.
- If the test period is truly representative of day-to-day operations, one can take the difference between actual and standard costs to indicate the extent of inefficiency or improper performance in the enterprise.

7. Computers are useful for preparing the menu pre-cost and abstract and for comparing actual and standard costs for an operating period.

Chapter 11 Exercises

1. What is standard cost? When will the standard cost of a portion differ from its actual cost?

    _____

    _____

    _____

L.O. 11.1

2. The information on the following page covers a one-week operating period for Ellie's Bar & Grill. The operation uses the daily comparison method for comparing actual and standard costs. Using Figure 11.1 on text page 251 as a guide, complete the menu pre-cost and abstract shown on the following page.

L.O. 11.2

3. Name three ways an undesirable forecasted food cost percent might be changed.

    • _____

    • _____

    • _____

L.O. 11.3

4. Complete the following formula:

    Actual costs − Standard costs = _____

L.O. 11.4

5. Managers at Ellie's Bar & Grill are considering the use of the periodic comparison method because of the large time investment needed for daily comparison. Using the information in question #1 and Figure 11.4 on text page 259 as a guide, prepare a periodic potential savings worksheet on a separate sheet of paper. Use $795 for your actual cost.

L.O. 11.5

6. As computers have become more common in foodservice operations, which means of comparing actual and standard food costs has become more widely used? Why?

    _____

    _____

    _____

L.O. 11.6

64

Exercise 2

Ellie's Bar and Grill

Menu Item	# Forecast	Forecast			Total Cost	Total Sales	# Sold	Actual			Total Cost	Total Sales
		Cost	S.P.	F.C. %				Cost	S.P.	F.C. %		
A	40	4.05	11.00				38	4.05	11.00			
B	100	2.75	8.50				99	2.75	8.50			
C	80	2.50	6.50				72	2.50	6.50			
D	50	3.00	9.00				50	3.00	9.00			

Chapter 11 Check-in

1. The agreed-upon cost of goods or services used to measure other costs is called
   - A. actual cost.
   - B. standard cost.
   - C. derived cost.
   - D. portion cost.

   L.O. 11.1

2. The left side of the menu pre-cost and abstract reflects which of the following?
   - A. Actual costs
   - B. Forecasted figures
   - C. Food cost percents
   - D. Sales prices

   L.O. 11.2

3. To complete the Total Cost column for the forecast side of the menu pre-cost and abstract, multiply the number of portion sales forecasted for any given item by the
   - A. food cost percent for that item.
   - B. actual cost for that item.
   - C. standard portion cost of that item.
   - D. sales price of that item.

   L.O. 11.2

4. One way to change an undesirable forecasted food cost percent is to
   - A. institute a total quality assurance program.
   - B. change sales prices.
   - C. hire additional employees.
   - D. lower contribution margins.

   L.O. 11.3

5. Which of the following indicates the level of food cost management will approve to achieve a given level of dollar sales?
   - A. Cost percent from a previous period
   - B. Forecasted cost percent
   - C. Actual cost percent
   - D. Potential savings

   L.O. 11.2

6. Actual cost for Tuesday at Benny's Buffet was $895, while sales for the day were $3,200. What was the actual cost percent for Tuesday?
   - A. 28.0%
   - B. 31.4%
   - C. 33.5%
   - D. 39.2%

   L.O. 11.2

7. The difference between actual costs and standard costs is called
   - A. cumulative costs.
   - B. potential savings.
   - C. perfected difference.
   - D. maintained expense.

   L.O. 11.4

8. When performing a periodic comparison, it is usually advisable to select test periods
   - A. carefully.
   - B. similar to the current period.
   - C. before the fact.
   - D. at random.

   L.O. 11.5

9. A portion of the potential savings figure at Max & Jenny's can be traced to overproduction. By eliminating the overproduction while keeping other costs in line, management should see a(n)

    A. increase in customer satisfaction.
    B. decrease in profit.
    C. increase in employee productivity.
    D. reduction in excessive costs.

    L.O. 11.5

10. Which of the following is much more widely used to compare actual to standard costs with the increasing availability of computers in the foodservice workplace?

    A. Standard portion sizes
    B. Corrective action
    C. Meat tags
    D. Menu pre-cost and abstract

    L.O. 11.6

CHAPTER 12

CONTROLLING FOOD SALES

Learning Objectives

12.1   List and explain the three goals of sales control.

12.2   List and describe eight determinants of customer restaurant selection.

12.3   Describe the two principal means of maximizing profits.

12.4   Explain the three most common methods of establishing menu prices.

12.5   Describe the two principal means of selling products effectively in a restaurant.

12.6   List and explain the five most important elements of menu preparation.

12.7   Explain attempts by management to maximize profits by establishing sales techniques for use by the sales force.

12.8   Explain the importance of revenue control.

12.9   List and explain the three standards established to achieve the goals of revenue control.

12.10 List and describe the five standard procedures for controlling revenue.

12.11 Describe two ways in which computers are used in revenue control.

12.12 Explain the importance of menu engineering as an analytical tool.

12.13 Describe how to complete a menu engineering worksheet, interpret the results, and suggest various possible changes to improve profit.

Chapter 12 Study Outline

1. There are three principal goals of sales control: optimizing the number of sales, maximizing profit, and controlling revenue.

2. To optimize the number of sales, it is important to consider how customers select restaurants. The following are important for most people: location, menu item differentiation, price acceptability, decor, portion sizes, product quality, service standards, and menu diversity.

3. There are two principal means for maximizing profit: pricing products properly and selling those products effectively.

- Cost is usually the most significant consideration in establishing the sales price for any menu item. Another important consideration is the desire to maximize sales.
- Three basic approaches to setting menu prices include matching competitors' prices, calculating prices from costs and cost percents, and adding desired contribution margins to portion costs.
- A restaurant has two principal means for selling products effectively: the menu and the sales techniques used by the staff.
- The five most important elements of menu development are layout and design, variety, item arrangement and location, descriptive language, and kitchen personnel and equipment.
- The second means for selling products effectively is to develop appropriate sales techniques to be used by servers, who represent the restaurant's sales force.
- In many restaurants, managers hold daily meetings with servers just before opening time to review the menu.
- Another technique is to train servers to suggest menu items.

4. To achieve effective control over revenue, management must establish standard procedures intended to ensure that food sales are documented (on guest checks, for example), priced correctly, and checked and verified daily.

- Numbered guest checks make it possible to assign responsibility for specific checks to particular employees by having employees sign for them.
- To control revenue, many restaurants use the dupe system.
- For proper revenue control, sales should always be recorded in a register, and each guest check should be endorsed by the register as the sale is recorded so the check is not reused.

5. Menu analysis provides a means for monitoring the effectiveness of efforts to maximize profits.

- Menu engineering is a technique used to evaluate a menu by assessing sales volume and contribution margin for each item and, thus, to evaluate individual menu items. Menu items can be identified as one of four possible combinations:
  - Star (high contribution margin and high volume)
  - Dog (low contribution margin and low volume)
  - Plowhorse (low contribution margin and high volume)
  - Puzzle (high contribution margin and low volume)

6. Computers play a key role in controlling revenue, such as developing a sales history, generating sales reports quickly while sales are in progress, and recording orders (thereby eliminating the need for guest checks and dupes).

Chapter 12 Exercises

Indicate whether each of the following statements is true (T) or false (F). If false, correct the statement.

_____1. Revenue control is the same as sales control.

_____

_____

L.O. 12.1

_____2. Having a good location is usually not necessary for volume business.

_____

_____

L.O. 12.2

_____3. A homogeneous product or service is so similar to another that customers do not have a preference and will purchase whichever costs less.

_____

_____

L.O. 12.2

_____4. The more homogeneous a menu item, the less price sensitive it is.

_____

_____

L.O. 12.2

_____5. Most restaurants find it necessary to have a broad range of items on the menu.

_____

_____

L.O. 12.2

_____6. The two general ways to maximize profit are to price products properly and to sell those products effectively.

_____

_____

L.O. 12.3

_____7. Cost is the only determinant of sales price.

_____

_____

L.O.12.3

_____8. Calculating prices from costs and cost percents is the most widely used approach to menu pricing.

_____

_____

L.O. 12.4

_____9. The primary sales tool in most restaurants is the menu.

_____

_____

L.O. 12.5

_____10. A good general menu should include at least five entrees.

_____

_____

L.O. 12.6

_____11. Menu items listed in the margins are seen first and make the greatest impression.

_____

_____

L.O. 12.6

_____12. A menu writer needs to be familiar with the kinds of equipment available in the kitchen.

_____

_____

L.O. 12.6

_____13. If a chef has prepared a limited quantity of a desirable fresh fish item not usually on the menu, the menu should be reprinted.

_____

_____

L.O. 12.7

_____14. One useful sales technique that many successful restaurateurs train their personnel to use is to encourage the selection of menu items or courses customers mention an interest in.

_____

_____

L.O. 12.7

_____15. Standards and standard procedures for revenue control are aimed at ensuring that all food served produces the maximum revenue for the enterprise.

_____

_____

L.O. 12.8

_____16. An establishment with excellent cost controls may be a financial failure without proper revenue control.

_____

_____

L.O. 12.8

_____17. Padded checks are more common in restaurants where the style of service is formal.

_____

_____

L.O. 12.9, 12.10

_____18. Two important aspects of hand-prepared guest checks are legibility and accuracy.

_____

_____

L.O. 12.9, 12.10

_____19. Food checkers are employed at a majority of restaurants to control against servers giving away food or undercharging for menu items.

_____

_____

L.O. 12.9, 12.10

_____20. Menu engineering provides a means for determining net receipts.

_____

_____

L.O. 12.12

_____21. If lemon chicken accounts for 300 portions out of the total portion sales for all 1,800 items, the menu mix percent is 18.2%.

_____

_____

L.O. 12.13

_____22. The menu CM on a menu engineering worksheet indicates the total of contribution margins provided by a particular menu item.

_____

_____

L.O. 12.13

_____23. The two CM categories on a menu engineering worksheet are H (homogeneous) and D (differentiated).

_____

_____

L.O. 12.13

_____24. A menu item that produces a low contribution margin but accounts for relatively high volume is called a "plowhorse."

_____

_____

L.O. 12.13

_____25. Menu items classified as "dogs" should be removed from the menu immediately.

_____

_____

L.O. 12.13

_____26. One of the most important uses of the computer as a sales control device is in eliminating the need for traditional guest checks and dupes.

_____

_____

L.O. 12.11

Chapter 12 Check-in

1. A collection of activities designed to ensure that each order placed by a customer results in appropriate revenue for the enterprise is called

   A. revenue control.
   B. sales control.
   C. profit maximization.
   D. sales optimization.

   L.O. 12.1

2. Unique menu items created to increase sales volume are referred to as

   A. homogenous products.
   B. signature items.
   C. engineered entrées.
   D. stars.

   L.O. 12.2

3. The sales prices for menu items are usually established by

   A. the chef.
   B. accountants.
   C. owners or managers.
   D. marketing personnel.

   L.O. 12.3

4. The most widely used approach to menu pricing is to

   A. calculate prices from costs and cost percents.
   B. add desired contribution margins to portion costs.
   C. extrapolate using regression analysis.
   D. match competitors' prices.

   L.O. 12.4

5. The primary sales tool in most restaurants is the

   A. waitstaff.
   B. host or hostess.
   C. comment card.
   D. menu.

   L.O. 12.5

6. Which of the following is true of menu preparation?

   A. Menu items should be listed in a simple, straightforward manner.
   B. All menu entrées should be featured in larger type than appetizers, drinks, and desserts.
   C. A reasonable range of entrée prices should be included.
   D. Kitchen equipment need not be considered.

   L.O. 12.6

7. How do pre-shift meetings with managers and servers just before opening time benefit customers?

   A. If the operation opens late, servers often offer free appetizers to customers.
   B. The meetings increase the chance that customers will get accurate information about menu offerings.
   C. Daily specials are posted where all customers can see them.
   D. The meetings let customers know that managers are watching the performance of the employees.

   L.O. 12.7

8. Failure to account for all food served to customers and employees will result in

   A. distortion of the cost-to-sales ratio.
   B. theft.
   C. customer dissatisfaction.
   D. employee harmony.

   L.O. 12.8

9. Guest checks assigned to servers one at a time are known as

   A. padded checks.
   B. unpadded checks.
   C. sequential checks.
   D. individual checks.

   L.O. 12.9, 12.10

10. Dividing the number of units sold by the total number of units sold for all items yields which of the following?

    A. Menu CM
    B. Menu mix percent
    C. Menu cost
    D. Menu revenue

    L.O. 12.13

CHAPTER 13

BEVERAGE PURCHASING CONTROL

Learning Objectives

13.1   List and describe the three principal classifications of beverages.

13.2   Identify two broad classifications of beers and distinguish between them.

13.3   Identify the three color classifications of wine.

13.4   Describe the fermentation process and explain its significance in the making of alcoholic beverages.

13.5   Explain the purpose of the distillation process.

13.6   Explain the difference between call brands and pouring brands.

13.7   List the primary purposes for establishing beverage purchasing controls.

13.8   Identify the principal factors one must consider before establishing quality standards for beverages.

13.9   Identify eight principal factors used to establish quantity standards for beverages.

13.10   Explain the difference between license states and control states.

13.11   Identify the two principal methods for determining order quantities and calculate order quantities using both methods.

13.12   Describe one standard procedures for processing beverage orders in larger hotels and restaurants.

13.13   Describe the use of computers to determine order quantities for beverages.

Chapter 13 Study Outline

1. Beverages can be divided into two groups: alcoholic and nonalcoholic.

   - Alcoholic beverages are divided into three categories: beers, wines, and spirits.
   - Two broad classifications of beer are lager beers and ales.
   - Wines are normally classified as red, white, or rosé. These color classifications are not the only means for identifying wines. They can also be classified as follows:
     - Varietal wines
     - Brand name wines
     - Geographic wines
     - Generic wines
   - There are several types of wines and wine-based beverages that are different from regular wines, including sparkling wines, fortified wines, wine coolers, and blush wines.

2. For control purposes, the responsibility for purchasing beverages should be assigned to one employee not directly engaged in either the preparation or sale of drinks.

3. The purposes of beverage-purchasing controls are to maintain an appropriate supply of ingredients for producing beverage products, to ensure that the quality of ingredients purchased is appropriate for their intended use, and to ensure that ingredients are purchased at optimum prices.

4. For beverage purchasing, standards must be developed for quality, quantity, and price.

   - Before establishing quality standards for alcoholic beverages, a foodservice manager must first weigh a number of considerations, including product cost, customer preferences, and product popularity, among others.
   - Alcoholic beverages purchased for bars are classified as either call brands (asked for by name) or pouring brands.
   - The principal factors used to establish quantity standards for beverage purchasing are:
     - Frequency of placing orders
     - Storage space available
     - Funds available for inventory purchases
     - Delivery schedules set by purveyors
     - Minimum-order requirements set by purveyors
     - Price discounts for volume orders
     - Price specials available
     - Limited availability of some items
   - All beverage purchases should be made at optimum prices. Pricing varies, depending on whether the buyer is in a license state or a control state.

5. The next step is to establish standard procedures to determine order quantities and to process orders.

   - There are two basic methods for determining order quantities: the periodic order method (based on fixed order dates and variable order quantities) and the perpetual order method (based on variable order dates and fixed order quantities).

6. Operations should establish a purchasing routine that requires formal written purchase orders.

7. On-the-job training is effective for training employees on standard procedures for beverage purchasing.

8. There are several possibilities for monitoring employees.

   - With the periodic order method, the employee can take the physical inventory using a standard form created by management.
   - With the perpetual method, managers examine the perpetual inventory cards to see that orders have been placed properly.

9. Computers can be used to remove much of the tedious work associated with determining purchase quantities. Managers can use a computer to maintain records of purchases and to print reports showing, for example, total purchases of each beverage in inventory in units, dollars, or both, or totals for categories of items.

Chapter 13 Exercises

1. a. Name three classifications of alcoholic beverages.

   - _____

   - _____

   - _____

L.O. 13.1

   b. Into what groupings can each of the classifications be further divided?

   _____

   _____

   _____

L.O. 13.2, 13.3

   c. In general, how is each category of alcoholic beverages produced?

   _____

   _____

   _____

L.O. 13.4, 13.5

d. What are nonalcoholic beverages used with alcoholic beverages to produce mixed drinks called? Name five examples.

_____

- _____
- _____
- _____
- _____
- _____

2. Distillation is the process by means of which alcohol is removed from a fermented liquid.
   a. What term is used to express the alcoholic content of a distillate?

   _____

   b. Which scale is used to the measure alcoholic content of a distillate?

   _____

   c. How would a beverage that is 50% alcohol be described?

   _____

   d. How is a distillate's proof related to its clarity?

   _____

L.O. 13.5

3. Which of the following are purposes of beverage-purchasing controls? Check all that apply.
   _____a. To ensure that ingredients are purchased at optimum prices
   _____b. To ensure that the quality of ingredients purchased is appropriate for their intended use
   _____c. To distinguish between call brands and pouring brands
   _____d. To maximize profits
   _____e. To maintain an appropriate supply of ingredients for producing beverage products

L.O. 13.7

4. Explain the difference between call brands and pouring brands. How does the use of call brands and pouring brands tie in with establishing quality standards?

    _____

    _____

    _____

L.O. 13.6

5. When purchasing beverages, a manager must consider various factors. Identify each of the following as most likely a quality factor (QUAL) or a quantity factor (QUAN).

    _____a. Customer preferences

    _____b. Order placement frequency

    _____c. Price discounts for volume orders

    _____d. Storage space availability

    _____e. Product popularity

    _____f. Limited availability of some items

    _____g. Purveyor delivery schedule

    _____h. Product cost

    _____i. Availability of funds

    _____j. Availability of price specials

    _____k. Minimum order requirements

L.O. 13.8, 13.9

6. Explain how beverage purchasing is done in a license state and in a control state.

    _____

    _____

    _____

L.O. 13.10

7. Distinguish between the periodic order method and the perpetual order method in determining quantities. Explain how each method works by giving an example.

    _____

    _____

    _____

L.O. 13.11

8. The Palace Hotel, a large, full-service operation in a major metropolitan city, requires purchase orders to be made up in quadruplicate. Where does each copy go and for what reason?

_____

_____

_____

_____

L.O. 13.12

9. Why might a beverage buyer prefer to use a database program rather than a spreadsheet when determining purchase quantities for beverages? Why might the buyer prefer a spreadsheet?

_____

_____

_____

L.O. 13.13

Chapter 13 Check-in

1. Which of the following is produced by the fermentation of malted grain?
   A. Beer
   B. Wine
   C. Spirits
   D. Nonalcoholic beverages
   L.O. 13.1, 13.4

2. Lager beer
   A. includes porter and stout.
   B. is typically stronger than wine coolers.
   C. is the type most commonly consumed in the United States.
   D. has a higher alcohol content than ale.
   L.O. 13.2

3. The color of a wine is determined by the manner in which it is processed and the
   A. alcohol content.
   B. variety of grape used.
   C. place of the wine's origin.
   D. amount of spirits added.
   L.O. 13.3

4. The alcoholic content of a distillate is stated in terms of
   A. par stock.
   B. cost.
   C. turnover.
   D. proof.
   L.O. 13.5

5. Call brands of liquor are

    A. requested by name by customers.
    B. always stored on the top shelf.
    C. sold at lower prices.
    D. sold in license states only.

L.O. 13.6

6. One purpose of beverage-purchasing controls is to ensure that ingredients are purchased

    A. above cost.
    B. at optimum prices.
    C. from favored vendors.
    D. evenly throughout the year.

L.O. 13.7

7. Which of the following should be considered when establishing quality standards for beverage purchasing?

    A. Storage space availability
    B. Product popularity
    C. Minimum order requirements
    D. Vendors' delivery schedules

L.O. 13.8, 13.9

8. The state government sells some or all alcoholic beverages through its own network of stores in which of the following?

    A. License state
    B. Dry state
    C. Certified state
    D. Control state

L.O. 13.10

9. Ordering variable amounts of beverages at fixed order dates is referred to as the

    A. par stock method.
    B. reorder time.
    C. periodic order method.
    D. perpetual order method.

L.O. 13.11

10. If the periodic method is used, it is easy to develop a worksheet for calculating purchase quantities using a(n)

    A. DSL connection.
    B. outside auditor.
    C. spreadsheet program.
    D. database program.

L.O. 13.13

CHAPTER 14

BEVERAGE RECEIVING, STORING, AND ISSUING CONTROL

Learning Objectives

14.1   Identify the objectives of controls for receiving, storing, and issuing beverages.

14.2   List and explain the various standards necessary for establishing control over beverage receiving, storing, and issuing.

14.3   Describe the standard receiving procedure for beverages.

14.4   List the types of information contained in a beverage receiving report and explain the report's use.

14.5   Describe two means for maintaining security in beverage storage facilities.

14.6   Describe the procedures used to organize beverage storage facilities.

14.7   Describe the effect of temperature, humidity, light, handling techniques, and storing methods on the shelf life of beverages.

14.8   List the three types of bars and describe their differences.

14.9   Define a *requisition system* and describe its use in beverage control.

14.10 Compare the techniques for receiving, storing, and issuing beverages used in small restaurants and bars with those used in large hotels and restaurants.

14.11 Compare methods used for training employees for beverage receiving, storing, and issuing in large and small properties.

14.12 List and describe three means of monitoring the performance of employees responsible for receiving, storing, and issuing beverages.

14.13 Describe the use of computers in beverage receiving, storing, and issuing control.

Chapter 14 Study Outline

1. The primary goal of receiving control is to ensure that deliveries received conform exactly to orders placed. In practice, this means that beverage deliveries must be compared to beverage orders with respect to quantity, quality, and price.

   - Standard procedures must be established to ensure that standards will be met. Basic standard procedures for receiving beverages include:
     - Maintaining an up-to-date file of all beverage orders placed.
     - Comparing the record of the order to the delivery driver's invoice.
     - Checking brands, dates, or both, and counting or weighing goods delivered before the driver leaves.
     - Comparing the invoice to the order.
     - Checking deliveries for any broken or leaking containers and any bottles with broken seals or missing labels.
     - Noting all discrepancies between delivered goods and those ordered on the invoice itself.
     - Signing the original invoice to acknowledge receipt of the goods. Retain a copy for internal records.
     - Recording the invoice on the beverage receiving report.
     - Notifying the person responsible for storing that a delivery has been received.

2. Storing control is established in beverage operations to achieve three important objectives: to prevent pilferage, ensure accessibility when needed, and preserve quality.

   - There are two ways to maintain security: assign the responsibility for the stored items to a single employee and keep the beverage-storage facility locked at all times.
   - To ensure accessibility of product when needed, the storage facility must be organized so that each individual brand and product is stored in the same location.
   - To preserve quality, maintain the appropriate temperature, humidity, and light during storage.

3. Issuing control is established to achieve two objectives: to ensure the timely release of beverages from inventory in the needed quantities and to prevent the misuse of alcoholic beverages between release from inventory and delivery to the bar.

   - To achieve these objectives, management must establish two standards: issue quantities must be set, and beverages must be issued to authorized persons only.
   - There are three types of bars: front bars, service bars, and special-purpose bars.
   - The standard procedures for issuing beverages are to establish par stocks for bars and to set up a requisition system.
     - For bars, par stock is the precise quantity of an item that must be on hand at all times for each beverage at the bar.
     - Both the names of the beverages and the quantities of each issued should be recorded on bar requisition forms.

4. Training cannot proceed effectively without carefully conceived standards and standard procedures.

5. The job performance of employees who receive, store, and issue beverages must be monitored.
    - Perhaps the most common monitoring technique in beverage operations is a monthly physical inventory of stored beverages and a determination of cost of beverages sold.
    - At the same time, managers can monitor adherence to standard procedures by verifying quantities received and issued, reviewing the organization of the storage facility, and evaluating the temperature and cleanliness of the storage area and the manner in which the beverages are stored.
    - Managers can also spot-check employees' work, observe employees over closed-circuit television, or verify receiving records before beverages are sent to storage.
6. Computers can be used for record keeping, as well as for the maintenance of a perpetual beverage inventory.

Chapter 14 Exercises

1. Indicate whether each of the following objectives or standards applies to receiving (R), storing (S), or issuing (I).

    _____a. The quantity of an item delivered must equal the quantity ordered.

    _____b. Ensure the timely release of beverages from inventory in the needed quantities.

    _____c. Prevent pilferage.

    _____d. Establish par stocks for bars.

    _____e. The quality of an item delivered must be the same as the quality ordered.

    _____f. Preserve quality.

    _____g. Set up a requisition system.

    _____h. Ensure accessibility when needed.

    _____i. The price on the invoice for each item delivered should be the same as the price listed when the order was placed.

L.O. 14.1, 14.2

2. The standard procedures for receiving beverages at Chez Pierre mirror those discussed in the textbook. Mauricio, the operation's receiving clerk, has just accepted an order. He has checked the brands and dates of the beverages and has counted and weighed all delivered goods. He has also signed the original invoice and returned the signed copy to the delivery driver. Finally, he has notified Max, the person responsible for storing beverages, that a delivery has been received.

   a. What has Mauricio forgotten to do?

   _____

   _____

   _____

L.O. 14.3

   b. What should Mauricio use to summarize the invoices for all beverages received today?

   _____

   _____

L.O. 14.4

   c. One month later, Max stops working at Chez Pierre to get a formal education in hospitality management. He was the operation's employee with access to the beverage-storage facility. What should Chez Pierre managers do to ensure the security of the storeroom?

   _____

   _____

   _____

L.O. 14.5

   d. At Chez Pierre, customers' orders are given to the bartender by the waitstaff, who serve the drinks to the customers. What kind of bar is this?

   _____

L.O. 14.8

3. Name four procedures used to organize beverage-storage facilities.

   - _____

   - _____

   - _____

   - _____

L.O. 14.6

4. Indicate whether each of the following statements is true (T) or false (F).

_____a. Spirits can be stored indefinitely at normal room temperatures without harming product quality.

_____b. Red wines should be stored at about 30°F.

_____c. Beer that has once been chilled should be kept chilled to maintain quality.

_____d. The degree of moisture in the air is of significance only for beer.

_____e. Bottled wines should be kept away from natural light.

_____f. Corked beverages can be safely stored in an upright position.

_____g. Canned and bottled beers usually are not shelved.

L.O. 14.7

5. What is a requisition system? What role does the bar requisition form play in the system?

_____

_____

_____

L.O. 14.9

6. Small restaurants and bars and those in large hotels and restaurants use various, contrasting techniques with respect to beverage receiving, storing, and issuing.

a. Name one procedure or standard that might be employed by a large, rather than a small, operation.

_____

_____

L.O. 14.10

b. Contrast the methods often used to train employees in beverage receiving, storing, and issuing in small and large operations.

_____

_____

_____

L.O. 14.11

7. Name three means of monitoring the performance of employees responsible for receiving, storing, and issuing beverages.

- _____

- _____

- _____

L.O. 14.12

8. Name three uses of computers for the maintenance of various important records related to beverages.

- _____

- _____

- _____

L.O. 14.13

Chapter 14 Check-in

1. To ensure that deliveries received conform exactly to orders placed is the primary goal of
   A. serving.
   B. storing.
   C. issuing.
   D. receiving.
   L.O. 14.1

2. For bars, par stock is the
   A. precise quantity that must be on hand at all times.
   B. maximum quantity that may be on hand at any one time.
   C. exact quantity to be ordered.
   D. approximate quantity consumed.
   L.O. 14.2

3. There can be no effective receiving procedures without
   A. written records of the orders placed.
   B. satisfied repeat customers.
   C. quantity discounts and specials offered by purveyors.
   D. knowledgeable storeroom personnel.
   L.O. 14.3

4. Which of the following forms is prepared daily by the individual responsible for receiving beverages?
   A. Beverage receiving report
   B. Requisition
   C. Invoice
   D. Liquor identification number
   L.O. 14.4

88

5. It is most efficient for the security of a beverage-storage area to be assigned to
   A. one employee.
   B. two employees.
   C. three employees.
   D. however many employees are needed.
   L.O. 14.5

6. Stamping code numbers on bottles of alcoholic beverages
   A. is standard procedure in most mid-sized operations.
   B. serves as an incentive for theft.
   C. presupposes employee dishonesty.
   D. makes it impossible for an employee to claim that such a bottle is personal property.
   L.O. 14.6

7. Which wine needs to be stored at the coolest temperatures?
   A. Red
   B. White
   C. Rose
   D. Blush
   L.O. 14.7

8. At which type of bar do bartenders serve the public face to face?
   A. Service bars
   B. Front bars
   C. Standard bars
   D. Special-purpose bars
   L.O. 14.8

9. Which of the following is a highly structured method for controlling issues?
   A. Par stock system
   B. Dupe system
   C. Requisition system
   D. Perpetual system
   L.O. 14.9

10. The more complete a job description, the simpler the task of
    A. receiving.
    B. training.
    C. monitoring.
    D. evaluating.
    L.O. 14.11

CHAPTER 15

BEVERAGE PRODUCTION CONTROL

Learning Objectives

15.1   Identify the two primary objectives of beverage production control.

15.2   Describe the standards and standard procedures necessary for establishing control over beverage production.

15.3   List four devices used to standardize quantities of alcoholic beverages used in beverage production.

15.4   Describe the use of standardized glassware in beverage control and the importance of stipulating specific glassware for each drink.

15.5   Explain the significance of standard drink recipes in beverage control.

15.6   Calculate the standard cost of any drink, given a standard recipe and the current market prices of ingredients.

15.7   Calculate the standard cost-to-sales ratio for any drink, given its standard cost and sales price.

15.8   Determine the standard number of straight shots in bottles of various sizes, given the quantity standard for the straight shot.

15.9   Describe two approaches commonly used to train bartenders to follow established standards and standard procedures.

15.10   Explain why bar operations should be monitored frequently.

15.11   List four techniques for monitoring the performance of bartenders.

15.12   Identify three types of computer programs that can be used for maintaining standard drink recipes.

Chapter 15 Study Outline

1. The objectives of beverage production control are to:
   - Ensure that all drinks are prepared according to management's specifications.
   - Guard against excessive costs that can develop in the production process.
2. When standards are set for ingredients, proportions, and drink sizes, customers can have some reasonable assurance that a drink will meet expectations each time it is ordered.
   - Devices used for measuring standard quantities include shot glasses (plain or lined), jiggers, pourers, and automated dispensers.
   - Bartenders who free-pour measure quantity using only their own judgment and eyesight.
   - Standardizing the glassware helps to control the overall sizes of drinks, as well as establish portion control.
3. Standard recipes allow bar personnel to know the exact quantity of each ingredient to use in producing any given drink.
4. To simplify the task of determining standard costs of cocktails and other mixed drinks, many bar managers use standard recipe detail and cost cards, on which each ingredient is costed out and totaled.
5. Standard sale prices help ensure customer satisfaction, maintain a planned cost-to-sales ratio for each drink, and allow managers to plan and maintain acceptable levels of profit.
6. Bartenders must be trained to follow standards and standard procedures.
   - A suitable first step in training in most operations is to conduct an appropriate orientation to working in the establishment.
   - Actual training takes place at the specific workstation. The trainer explains the standards and basic procedures for producing drinks. This training is conducted at a time when it will not interfere with normal business, and the bartender is given ample opportunity to ask questions.
   - Alternatively, many large operations employ specialized personnel to prepare training and operation manuals.
7. One common approach to monitoring beverage production is to observe bartenders as they proceed with their daily work.
   - Observation can be done by a manager, a designated employee (such as a head bartender), individuals unknown to the bartenders, or closed-circuit television.
8. Computers can be used in beverage production to maintain standard drink-recipe files and to determine standard costs for drinks. Whether managers use a word processing, spreadsheet, or database program, maintaining standard recipes is both simpler and easier with a computer.

Chapter 15 Exercises

As the new beverage manager of Renee's Lounge, an upscale, mid-sized beverage operation located in a large hotel, you have been asked to analyze current operations and institute new practices if necessary.

1. What should be your primary objectives in establishing control over beverage production? Which standards will help you achieve them?

    _____

    _____

    _____

    _____

L.O. 15.1, 15.2

2. At the front bar, bartenders control the quantity of liquor in drinks with a pourer. Discuss the advantages and disadvantages of this measuring device.

    _____

    _____

    _____

    _____

L.O. 15.3

3. Cocktails are currently served in standard four-ounce glasses. Assess the operation's use of this glassware.

    _____

    _____

    _____

L.O. 15.4

4. Renee's does not use standard bar recipes, allowing bartenders the freedom to cater to customer tastes and requests. Would you recommend that standard recipes be used? Why or why not?

_____

_____

_____

L.O. 15.5

5. In examining the standard costs for straight drinks, you notice that Renee's records reflect prices from 1988.
   a. Calculate current costs given the following information:

Item	Bottle Size (ml)	Bottle Cost	Drink Size	Standard Cost
Dewar's	750	$17.95	1.5 ounces	
Nessie's Blended	1,000	$13.95	1.5 ounces	
Grant's	750	$14.95	1.5 ounces	
Bell's	750	$11.95	1.5 ounces	
Teacher's	1,000	$15.95	1.5 ounces	

   b. If management aims for a cost-to-sales ratio of 20%, how should each drink above be priced?

Item	Drink Price
Dewar's	
Nessie's Blended	
Grant's	
Bell's	
Teacher's	

L.O. 15.6–15.8

6. Managers at Renee's currently do not monitor employee performance.

   a. Why is such monitoring vital?

   _____

   _____

   _____

   b. What possible ways can performance be observed?

   _____

   _____

   _____

L.O. 15.10, 15.11

7. Which three kinds of computer programs can be used for maintaining standard drink recipes?

   • _____

   • _____

   • _____

L.O. 15.12

Chapter 15 Check-in

1. One objective of beverage production is to ensure that all drinks are prepared
   A. with the same amount of alcohol in each.
   B. according to customers' tastes and preferences.
   C. according to management's specifications.
   D. at the lowest possible cost.

   L.O. 15.1

2. When managers establish and maintain standards for beverage production, which of the following will remain constant?
   A. Total cost for all drinks across the board
   B. Contribution margin for each drink
   C. Standard drink recipes
   D. The cost-to-sales ratio for every portion of that drink

   L.O. 15.2

3. A double-ended, stainless steel measuring device, each end of which resembles a shot glass, is called a

    A. pourer.
    B. jigger.
    C. mixer.
    d. cocktail stirrer.

    L.O. 15.3

4. Many fine hotels and restaurants consider which of the following too small?

    A. Four-ounce cocktail glass
    B. Six-ounce cocktail glass
    C. Eight-ounce hi-ball glass
    D. Nine-ounce tulip champagne glass

    L.O. 15.4

5. Which of the following measures ensures that the exact quantity of each ingredient will be used in producing any given drink?

    A. Inventory valuation
    B. Standard drink recipe
    C. Bin card
    D. Monitoring of employee performance

    L.O. 15.5

6. If the purchase price of a bottle of alcohol is $14.25 and it contains 15.5 drinks, what is the standard cost of each drink?

    A. $0.73
    B. $0.88
    C. $0.92
    D. $1.09

    L.O. 15.6

7. If the cost for a 1.5 ounce drink of a particular brand of rum is $0.67 and management wants a cost-to-sales ratio of 30%, how should the drink be priced?

    A. $1.90
    B. $2.05
    C. $2.10
    D. $2.25

    L.O. 15.7

8. Which of the following is an appropriate first step in training beverage production employees in most operations?

    A. Conducting an orientation to working in the establishment
    B. Detailing the standard procedures established for replenishing supplies
    C. Providing the employees with training manuals that specify the standards and standard procedures established for every job in the organization
    D. Explaining the standards and standard procedures for producing drinks

    L.O. 15.9

9. Which of the following are most frequently used to monitor the performance of beverage production employees?

   A. Peer reporting systems
   B. Closed-circuit television systems
   C. Comments from customers
   D. Undercover detectives

L.O. 15.10

10. Which of the following would a manager find most helpful in managing his or her standard beverage information?

   A. Specialized software
   B. Word processing package
   D. Generic database package
   C. Generic accounting spreadsheet package

L.O. 15.12

CHAPTER 16

Learning Objectives

16.1 Identify the three general approaches to monitoring beverage operations.

16.2 Calculate value of liquor issued to a bar, bar inventory differential, and cost of liquor consumed.

16.3 Calculate cost of beverages sold and beverage cost percent, both daily and monthly.

16.4 Calculate daily and monthly costs and cost percents for wines, spirits, and beers separately.

16.5 Explain how to determine standard beverage cost for a given period.

16.6 List five possible reasons for differences between actual and standard beverage costs.

16.7 Calculate potential sales value per bottle for beverages sold by the straight drink.

16.8 Determine a mixed drink differential and use it to adjust potential sales values.

16.9 Calculate potential sales values by the average sales value method.

16.10 Calculate potential sales values by the standard deviation method.

16.11 Identify the formulas used to calculate beverage inventory turnover, and explain how the results of this calculation can be interpreted for maintaining appropriate inventory levels of spirits and beers.

16.12 Identify two types of computer programs that can be used in monitoring beverage operations.

16.13 Name the beverage monitoring methods for which computers are most necessary.

Chapter 16 Study Outline

1. There are three general approaches to monitoring beverage operations:

   - The cost approach—comparing cost of beverages sold with either actual cost or standard cost.
   - The liquid measure approach—comparing the number of ounces of beverages sold with the number of ounces consumed.
   - The sales value approach—comparing the potential sales value of beverages consumed with the actual sales revenue recorded.

2. It is useful to compare cost and sales figures on a regular basis to see if the planned cost-to-sales ratio is being maintained (cost approach).

   - Beverage cost is determined from inventory and purchase figures in the following manner:

	Opening beverage inventory
+	Beverage purchases this month
=	Total available for sale this month
−	Closing inventory this month
=	Value of beverages issued to the bar
+(−)	Inventory differential
=	Cost of beverages consumed

   - The inventory differential is the difference between the bar inventory value at the beginning of the month and its value at the end of the month.
   - Beverage cost percent can be calculated as follows:
     Beverage cost ÷ Beverage sales = Beverage cost percent.
   - Many managers go further in their calculations to get a more accurate picture. They take into account some or all of these adjustments:

   Add:

   Food to bar (directs)
   Storeroom issues
   Mixers

   Subtract:

   Cooking liquor
   Entertainment by managers or business promotion
   Special promotions

   - Some managers also prefer to separate the beverage cost figure into its three components: cost of spirits, cost of wines, and cost of beers.
   - The standard cost method is a better approach to evaluating beverage costs and judging the effectiveness of control procedures. This method requires detailed records of drink sales and considerable calculation. The difference between the actual and standard costs represents excessive cost. Some possible causes include breakage, pilferage, and failure to record revenue from sales.

3. The liquid measure approach (ounce-control method) is done using meters attached to bottles or computerized devices that dispense ingredients.

4. Another approach to controlling beverage operations is to determine the sales revenue that should be generated by each full bottle of liquor.
   - Procedures involving potential sales values require considerable time and calculation, and are generally performed only at very large operations. Three methods can be used:
     - The actual sales record method requires that potential sales values be established on the basis of sales of straight shots only and then adjusted daily or periodically by means of the mixed drink differential. These adjustments to the values of bottles issued and consumed are made after sales have taken place.
     - The average sales value method requires analyzing sales for a test period and determining weighted average values for bottles in advance, based on historical sales records.
     - The standard deviation method is a modification of the second method and is easier to use. It requires calculation of the difference between actual dollar sales and potential sales value of bottles consumed in the period. This difference, assumed to be attributable to mixed drinks sales, is expressed as a percentage of potential sales for the period and is used in succeeding periods to adjust potential sales.

5. Managers must establish a routine procedure for monitoring the adequacy of beverage inventories.
   - The following formulas can be used to calculate turnover rate:
     - (Opening inventory + Closing inventory) ÷ 2= Average inventory
     - Cost of beverages sold ÷ Average inventory = Turnover rate
   - Generally accepted monthly turnover rates are 1.5 for spirits and 2.0 for beer.

6. Any of the methods for monitoring beverage operations may be integrated into a computer-based control system.

Chapter 16 Exercises

The following month-end information is given for the Corner Restaurant and Pub:

Opening beverage inventory	$5,500
Beverage purchases	$8,400
Closing inventory	$6,000
Bar inventory value at the beginning of the month	$800
Bar inventory value at the end of the month	$300
Beverage sales	$31,750
Food to bar transfers	$300
Mixers	$500
Cooking liquor	$200
Special promotions	$300

1. Management wants to be able to compare cost and sales figures on a regular basis to see if the planned cost-to-sales ratio is being maintained. Which general approach to monitoring beverage operations should be used?

   _____

   _____

L.O. 16.1

2. What is the value of liquor issued to the bar?

   _____

L.O. 16.2

3. What is the beverage cost percent without adjustments?

   _____

L.O. 16.3

4. What is the beverage cost percent with adjustments?

   _____

L.O. 16.3

5. Why might the Corner's managers decide to calculate individual cost-to-sale ratios for spirits, wines, and beers?

_____

_____

_____

L.O. 16.4

6. Why might the managers want to make daily calculations rather than monthly ones?

_____

_____

_____

L.O. 16.4

7. Management has determined standard beverage cost for the last month and has discovered a significant difference between actual and standard cost.

    a. Explain the process by which the standard beverage cost was determined.

    _____

    _____

    _____

L.O. 16.5

    b. What are three possible reasons for the differences?

    • _____

    • _____

    • _____

L.O. 16.6

8. The Corner's standard drink of vodka is one-and-a-half ounces, and the pouring brand is issued in one-liter bottles. If the sales price for the standard drink is $4.50, what is the potential sales value of each issued bottle of the pouring brand?

    _____

L.O. 16.7

9. What are the three different methods for establishing sales values when calculating potential sales values for mixed drinks?

- _____

- _____

- _____

L.O. 16.8

10. The total ounces of gin sold for the month was 421.5, and total sales for gin were $1,250.00. What was the average sales value of each liter of gin under the average sales value method?

_____

L.O. 16.9

11. a. What was The Corner's beverage turnover rate?

_____

b. The rate calculated above is for the operation's entire beverage inventory. If it only represents monthly turnover rate for spirits inventory, is it too high, too low, or on target?

_____

c. If it only represents monthly turnover rate for beer inventory , is it too high, too low, or on target?

_____

L.O. 16.11

12. Almost any beverage operation's monitoring method can be integrated into a computer-based control system.

a. Which two types of computer programs can be used?

- _____

- _____

L.O. 16.12

b. Computers are most necessary for which beverage-monitoring methods?

_____

_____

_____

L.O. 16.13

Chapter 16 Check-in

1. Comparing the number of ounces of beverages sold to the number of ounces consumed is the basis for which of the following beverage monitoring approaches?

    A. Cost approach
    B. Average sales value method
    C. Liquid measure approach
    D. Standard deviation method

    L.O. 16.1

2. Opening beverage inventory plus beverage purchases for the month equals which of the following?

    A. Value of beverages issued to the bar
    B. Bar inventory differential
    C. Cost of beverages consumed
    D. Total available for sale this month

    L.O. 16.2

3. If beverage cost was $8,100 for the month at the Sushi Stop and sales were $32,110, what was the establishment's beverage cost percent?

    A. 19.4%
    B. 22.1%
    C. 24.0%
    D. 25.2%

    L.O. 16.3

4. Why do some managers prefer to separate the beverage cost figure into three components: cost of spirits, cost of wines, and cost of beers?

    A. Changes from one period to another are apparent in a single cost percent figure that includes all three.
    B. Analyzing the cost-to-sales ratio just once each month presents some problems.
    C. Cost-to-sales ratios for these three may differ significantly from one another.
    D. A single cost percent figure is precise and accurate.

    L.O. 16.4

5. What is the first step in calculating standard beverage cost for a given operating period?

    A. Multiply the number of sales of each type of drink by the standard cost of that drink.
    B. Add total standard costs for all drinks.
    C. Compare total standard cost to actual cost for the same period.
    D. Take corrective action if necessary.

    L.O. 16.5

6. Why might actual beverage cost differ excessively from standard beverage cost?

    A. Change in vendor
    B. Pilferage
    C. Price increase
    D. Volume discounts not applied by vendor

    L.O. 16.6

7. In establishing control procedures involving potential sales values for mixed drinks, the major challenge is to determine

    A. sales price.
    B. sales values.
    C. weighted average values.
    D. fixed cost.

L.O. 16.8

8. Which of the following depends on results determined during a test period when careful records are kept of the number of drinks sold of each type?

    A. Beverage sales control method
    B. Average sales value method
    C. Book inventory method
    D. Cost control method

L.O. 16.9

9. Which of the following requires the establishment of a test period during which the manager takes all appropriate steps to ensure strict employee adherence to all standards and standard procedures?

    A. Standard deviation method
    B. Inventory turnover
    C. Ounce-control method
    D. Actual sales record method

L.O. 16.10

10. The turnover rate for beer at Papa's Pizzeria is 1.8. Compared to generally accepted monthly turnover rates, this figure is

    A. on target.
    B. rounded.
    C. too high.
    D. too low.

L.O. 16.11

CHAPTER 17

Learning Objectives

17.1 List and explain the three goals of beverage sales control.

17.2 Identify five explanations given by customers for patronizing establishments that serve drinks.

17.3 Describe the specific steps that bar managers can take to attract particular market segments.

17.4 Describe two methods that can be sued to maximize profits in beverage operations.

17.5 Identify two important factors normally taken into account when establishing beverage sales prices.

17.6 Name ten work practices considered unacceptable at bars because they inhibit the ability of bar managers to institute effective revenue control.

17.7 Identify the two basic operating patterns for bars that help determine management's approach to revenue control.

17.8 Describe the essential features of a pre-check system.

17.9 List the advantages and disadvantages of automated bars compared to more traditional methods of mixing and pouring drinks.

17.10 Describe one common computerized beverage sales control system.

Chapter 17 Study Outline

1. There are three objectives of beverage sales control, and they have special considerations in bar operations: optimizing the number of sales, maximizing profit, and controlling revenue.

2. Optimizing the number of sales means engaging in activities that will increase the number of customers to the desired level.

   - People patronize bars and restaurants with bars to socialize, conduct business, eat, be entertained, and/or kill time.

3. Profit maximization is accomplished by establishing drink prices that will maximize gross profit and by influencing customers' selections.

   - Profit maximization is not accomplished by getting customers to buy more product.
   - Beverage ingredient costs and labor costs per dollar sale are both significantly lower than those for food, so they are not as important in establishing sales prices. Overhead costs typically account for a large percentage of total costs.
   - Market considerations that must be taken into account in establishing drink prices include average income in the area served, prices charged by the competition, special advantages offered by a specific location, and managers' desire to maintain exclusivity through pricing.

4. Revenue control is difficult to maintain when the bartender performs all functions, from taking the order to accepting payment.

   - Undesirable bartending practices include working with the cash drawer open, under-ringing sales, overcharging customers, overpouring, underpouring, diluting bottle contents, bringing one's own bottle into the bar, charging for drinks not served, and drinking on the job.
   - Effective revenue control requires that employees adhere strictly to standards and standard procedures and that the performance of bartenders be monitored by managers.
   - To help control revenue, many establishments use numbered guest checks.

5. Computerized sales control systems are becoming more common. With a typical system, an order is placed into the computer, and then the computer prints it out at the bar. The bartender makes the drinks, and the server picks them up. When appropriate, the server has the computer print out a check and collects the cash or receives and processes a credit card. At the end of the day, the bar manager prints a report showing sales for all servers.

Chapter 17 Exercises

Indicate whether each of the following statements is true (T) or false (F).

_____ 1. An individual's reasons for patronizing a beverage establishment usually do not change from day to day. (L.O. 17.2)

_____ 2. Most automated bar systems can accommodate customers' requests for drinks made according to recipes other than the standard recipes programmed. (L.O. 17.9)

_____ 3. The use of bars and lounges for business discussion is probably most common with sales personnel. (L.O. 17.3)

_____ 4. Revenue control is the single objective of beverage sales control. (L.O 17.1)

_____ 5. Airport cocktail lounges and bars are examples of establishments that cater to those who must kill time. (L.O. 17.3)

_____ 6. Increasing customer purchases is a useful approach for maximizing profits from beverage sales. (L.O. 17.4)

_____ 7. The consumption of alcohol is almost incidental for people who patronize beverage operations in order to socialize. (L.O. 17.2)

_____ 8. Dram shop laws require beverage establishment personnel to ask for identification to verify proof of legal drinking age.

_____ 9. Dishonest bartenders might dilute bottle contents with water. (L.O. 17.6)

_____ 10. Once a target segment has been identified, the major decisions concern portion sizes and selling prices. (L.O. 17.5)

_____ 11. Profit maximization can be accomplished by establishing drink prices that will maximize gross profit and by influencing customers' selections. (L.O. 17.4)

_____ 12. It is desirable to sell more drinks with high contribution margins and fewer drinks with low contribution margins. (L.O. 17.7)

_____ 13. In order to reduce the number of revenue-control problems, management must establish standards and standard procedures for bar operations. (L.O. 17.6)

_____ 14. Overhead costs and market considerations are of great importance in establishing drink prices. (L.O. 17.5)

_____ 15. People patronizing establishments serving alcoholic beverages are usually motivated by the desire to consume alcohol. (L.O. 17.2)

_____ 16. The owner or manager of a beverage operation must determine which market segment he intends to target. (L.O. 17.3)

_____ 17. A pre-check system incorporates at least one register that allows bartenders to record sales as drinks are served. (L.O. 17.8)

_____ 18. Profit maximization can be achieved by featuring and promoting selected drinks. (L.O. 17.4)

_____19. There is only one type of establishment that derives primary revenue from beverage sales and provides entertainment to attract customers to buy the beverages. (L.O. 17.4)

_____20. Ingredient costs and labor costs are not as important in establishing sales prices for beverages as they are for establishing food prices. (L.O. 17.5)

_____21. The void key records those drinks rejected by customers or unserved because customers walked out. (L.O. 17.10)

_____22. When visual monitoring of the bartender is impossible or impractical, some degree of control is possible by eliminating the use of numbered guest checks. (L.O. 17.8)

_____23. Working with the cash drawer open makes it possible for dishonest employees to make sales transactions without recording the sales in the register. (L.O. 17.6)

_____24. A computerized sales-control system typically uses code numbers that can identify hundreds of drinks. (L.O. 17.10)

_____25. Underpouring is a technique adopted by bartenders who selectively overpour. (L.O. 17.6)

_____26. Many customers patronize food and beverage establishments primarily to eat, ordering alcoholic beverages as enhancements to their meals. (L.O. 17.2)

Chapter 17 Check-in

1. In beverage operations, optimizing the number of sales means engaging in activities that will
   A. increase the number of customers to the desired level.
   B. increase the number of drinks purchased by customers.
   C. decrease excessive costs.
   D. decrease the number of unproductive employees.
   L.O. 17.1

2. What is probably the most significant factor motivating those who patronize beverage operations?
   A. Conducting business
   B. Socializing
   C. Eating
   D. Seeking entertainment
   L.O. 17.2

3. Each subgroup of customers is called a
   A. guest cluster.
   B. sales group.
   C. market segment.
   D. seat.
   L.O. 17.3

4. Which of the following hold a serving establishment and the server financially liable for damages if any employee in the operation has served an alcoholic drink to an intoxicated person who, in turns, causes harm to a third party?
   A. Control states
   B. Dram shop laws
   C. Bans on "happy hours"
   D. DUI laws
   L.O. 17.4

5. Which of the following is a primary determinant of drink prices?

   A. Overhead costs
   B. Ingredient cost
   C. Labor cost
   D. Sales volume

   L.O. 17.5

6. Dishonest bar employees can steal the difference between the cash in the register drawer and the sales recorded on the tape by

   A. overpouring.
   B. under-ringing guest sales.
   C. undercharging customers.
   D. drinking on the job.

   L.O. 17.6

7. When visual monitoring methods are impractical, a degree of control is possible by the use of

   A. bin cards.
   B. numbered guest checks.
   C. a physical inventory.
   D. an automated system.

   L.O. 17.7

8. Registers that allow bartenders to record sales as drinks are served and to accumulate the sales to any one customer on one check are part of

   A. guest-check systems.
   B. pre-check systems.
   C. profit-maximization systems.
   D. automated systems.

   L.O. 17.8

9. Which of the following is an advantage to automated systems?

   A. Possibilities for charging incorrect prices are completely eliminated.
   B. Customers enjoy the "experience" of watching their drinks prepared by a machine.
   C. The proportions of ingredients are exactly the same each time a given drink is prepared.
   D. The quantity of each ingredient is estimated by the system.

   L.O. 17.9

10. What is one common time-saving feature when servers use a computerized sales control system?

   A. Servers can collect payment directly from customers.
   B. Servers can pick up drink orders from the service bar.
   C. Servers can use nicknames instead of their full names.
   D. Three- or four-digit code numbers are used in place of drink names.

   L.O. 17.10

CHAPTER 18

Learning Objectives

18.1 Define *employee compensation* and list the principal types of compensation common in food and beverage operations.

18.2 Explain the difference between direct and indirect compensation.

18.3 Explain why each of the following is a determinant of labor cost or labor cost percent: labor turnover rate; training; labor legislation; labor contracts; use of part-time staff; outsourcing; sales volume; location; equipment; layout; preparation; service; menu; hours of operation; weather; and competent management.

18.4 Explain why labor costs and labor cost percentages vary from one establishment to another.

18.5 Explain why the minimizing of dollar wages is not the same as labor cost control.

18.6 Define *labor cost control*.

Chapter 18 Study Outline

1. There are two forms of current compensation: direct (salaries, wages, tips, bonuses, commissions) and indirect (paid vacations, health benefits, life insurance, free meals, etc.).

2. The following are determinants of total labor costs and labor cost percents:

   - Labor turnover rate
   - Training
   - Labor legislation
   - Labor contracts
   - Use of part-time staff
   - Outsourcing
   - Sales volume
   - Location
   - Equipment
   - Layout
   - Preparation
   - Service
   - Menu
   - Hours of operation
   - Weather
   - Competent management

3. The impact of the various determinants varies considerably from one establishment to another.

4. Labor cost control is a process used by managers to direct, regulate, and restrain employees' actions in order to obtain desired levels of performance at appropriate levels of cost.

   • Labor cost control cannot be achieved by merely reducing payroll costs.

Chapter 18 Exercises

1. Indicate whether each of the following is direct compensation (D), indirect compensation (I), or deferred compensation (DEF).

   _____a. Wages   _____g. Salary

   _____b. Bonus   _____h. Social Security

   _____c. Paid vacation   _____i. Life insurance

   _____d. Right to use recreational facilities   _____j. Gratuities

            _____k. Health benefits

   _____e. Meals   _____l. Commission

   _____f. Pension benefits   _____m. Living accommodations

L.O. 18.1, 18.2

2. Explain how management's competence affects the cost of labor.

_____

_____

_____

L.O. 18.3

3. Why do labor costs vary from one foodservice establishment to another?

_____

_____

_____

L.O. 18.4

4. Indicate whether or not you agree with the following statement. State the reasons for your opinion.

   Minimizing dollar wages is an effective way to control labor costs.

   _____

   _____

   _____

L.O. 18.5, 18.6

Chapter 18 Check-in

1. All forms of pay and other rewards going to employees as a result of their employment is referred to as

   A. commission.
   B. promotion
   C. compensation.
   D. salary.

   L.O. 18.1

2. Which of the following is not paid from an employer's funds, but is considered compensation in the eyes of the law?

   A. Salary
   B. Gratuities
   C. Wages
   D. Bonuses

   L.O. 18.2

3. Paid vacation is an example of which of the following?

   A. Deferred compensation
   B. Direct compensation
   C. Indirect compensation
   D. Future compensation

   L.O. 18.2

4. Compared to other industries, the labor turnover rate in the foodservice industry is

   A. comparable.
   B. lower.
   C. higher.
   D. variable.

   L.O. 18.3

5. State legislatures have the power to mandate

   A. labor contracts.
   B. the use of part-time staff.
   C. higher minimum wages for employees than those established by Congress.
   D. training requirements.

   L.O. 18.3

6. The presence of labor contracts usually means that employee wages are

   A. similar to no union being present.
   B. lower than the national average.
   C. higher than if there was no union.
   D. lower than if there was no union.

   L.O. 18.3, 18.4

7. Arranging to have work done on a contract basis by outside organizations rather than by full-time employees is called
   A. job rotation.
   B. scheduling.
   C. minimizing.
   D. outsourcing.

   L.O. 18.3

8. Bad weather typically
   A. encourages potential customers to venture out to restaurants.
   B. discourages potential customers to venture out to restaurants.
   C. increases sales volume in hotel dining rooms.
   D. has no effect on patronage.

   L.O. 18.3

9. Hiring a full staff of employees at minimum wage is likely to
   A. lead to high-quality products.
   B. result in low labor turnover.
   C. create customer satisfaction.
   D. minimize only immediate labor cost.

   L.O. 18.5

10. The process used by managers to direct and regulate employee's actions in order to obtain desired levels of performance at appropriate levels of cost is called
    A. monitoring.
    B. management.
    C. productivity review.
    D. labor cost control.

    L.O. 18.6

CHAPTER 19

Learning Objectives

19.1   Explain the meaning and significance of quality and quantity standards in labor control.

19.2   Identify the three steps used to establish standards and standard procedures for employees.

19.3   Explain the need for an organizational plan.

19.4   Describe an organization chart.

19.5   Define the phrase *job description*.

19.6   Define the phrase *job analysis*, and explain its importance developing job descriptions.

19.7   Identify the three parts of a job description.

19.8   Define the phrase *job specification*, and explain its importance in making employment decisions.

19.9   Explain the difference between variable cost personnel and fixed cost personnel.

19.10 Explain how records of business volume are used in scheduling.

19.11 Explain the difference between the scheduling of variable cost personnel and the scheduling of fixed cost personnel.

19.12 Describe how to prepare an hourly schedule for variable cost personnel using records of business volume.

19.13 Describe how to develop performance standards based on a test period.

19.14 Explain how to determine appropriate staffing levels for an establishment, given a table of standard staffing requirements and a sales forecast.

19.15 Explain the use of computers and electronic cash registers in developing records of business volume.

Chapter 19 Study Outline

1. The three kinds of standards used in labor cost control are quality, quantity, and cost.
   - Before developing quality standards for employee performance, a manager must first have in mind a clear and detailed understanding of the establishment.
   - Once appropriate quality standards have been established, corresponding quantity standards must be developed.
   - The majority of foodservice operators are not able to use assembly-line techniques.
2. Establishing standards and standard procedures for employees requires organizing the enterprise, preparing job descriptions, and scheduling employees.
   - Before creating job descriptions, owners and managers must establish an organizational plan and prepare an organization chart.
   - The two most common methods of job analysis are interviewing workers and supervisors to obtain information and observing workers as they perform their jobs. The interviews and observations are designed to provide information about the following:
     - Job objectives
     - Specific tasks required to achieve objectives
     - Performance standards
     - Knowledge and skills necessary
     - Education and experience required
   - Job descriptions should explain what is to be done, as well as when and where. A job description typically has three parts:
     (1) Heading with job title, department, and other pertinent information
     (2) Summary of duties
     (3) List of the specific duties assigned to the job

3. There are two classifications of employees: variable-cost and fixed-cost personnel.
    *   One very important step managers should take before scheduling employees is to keep records of business volume. Daily tallies of the number of covers served can be prepared from a sales history, guest checks, or electronic cash registers. With data collected over a judicious period, business volume can be forecasted with some reasonable degree of accuracy.
    *   The first step in using tallies is to tabulate the hourly volume of business for a series of days. The next step is to translate the raw numbers into a graph that reflects the hourly periods of the operating day.
    *   A preliminary step in the scheduling of variable-cost employees is determining the types and numbers of employees needed at given levels of business volume. These are used to develop staffing tables. Staffing tables for variable-cost employees are estimates of the numbers of these employees required at various levels of business volume, given the quality and quantity standards established for their work.
    *   Before fixed-cost personnel can be scheduled with any degree of certainty, the manager must determine the specific requirements of each job. These schedules remain fairly constant.
4. Performance standards developed from records kept during a test period take both quantity and quality standards for work into account.
    *   A test period of a particular number of days or weeks is established for gathering data. During this period, detailed sales records are kept, indicating the number of covers served per day or per meal, depending on the type of establishment being analyzed. Evaluations are made by managers about the efficiency of the employees.
5. Once appropriate charts relating numbers of personnel to numbers of covers sold have been prepared for a test period and the manager has a record of sales volume, numbers of variable-cost employees working, and his or her own personal estimates of employees' efficiency, it is time to develop a table of standard staffing requirements for variable-cost personnel at several levels of business volume.
    *   Management can develop tables of standard work hours for all job categories at various levels of business activity.
    *   The development of standard work hours makes possible the development of standard labor costs. This may be done by simply multiplying the number of standard work hours required to perform a given volume of work by the hourly wage paid to those performing the work.

Chapter 19 Exercises

Blake, the new human resources manager for a mid-sized pizza chain, has gone through the company manual and highlighted several sections that do not seem quite right. On the page below, correct the sections Blake has flagged. Use a red pen if possible, and be sure that your corrections are legible.

ESTABLISHING STANDARDS AND STANDARD PROCEDURES

- Managers should follow this sequential order: (1) establish quantity standards; (2) develop a clear and detailed understanding of the establishment; (3) determine quality standards. (L.O. 19.1)

- In the restaurant business, production has to be linked to long-term demand because most food and beverage products can be stored for long periods of time. (L.O. 19.1)

- Establishing standards and standard procedures for employees requires two steps: preparing job descriptions and scheduling employees. (L.O. 19.2)

- Once owners or managers have thought in terms of specific jobs, they can develop the basic idea of the nature and scope of the operation. (L.O. 19.3)

- A standard staffing requirements worksheet shows the positions and describes reporting relationships within an organization. (L.O. 19.4)

PREPARING JOB DESCRIPTIONS

- Job analysis involves the creation of a chart that shows positions and describes reporting relationships. (L.O. 19.6)

- The information needed for job analysis (in this existing operation) is based on managers' previous experience in the industry. Information provided should focus on job objectives and education and experience required. (L.O. 19.6)

- Job descriptions tend to pose questions rather than answer them. They serve to outline the qualifications needed to perform a job. (L.O. 19.5)

- The three parts of a job description are those that answer the questions, *What is to be done?*, *When is it done?*, and *Where is it done?* (L.O. 19.7)

- A job description also describes the specific skills needed for a given job. (L.O. 19.8)

SCHEDULING EMPLOYEES

- The best way to schedule employees is to examine staffing levels from recent weeks and then to decide whether or not the level of staffing was sufficient to meet customers' needs. (L.O. 19.10)

- Fixed-cost personnel have schedules that are linked to business volume. Variable-cost personnel are those whose schedules are unrelated to business volume. (L.O. 19.9)

- Among the variable-cost personnel in a foodservice operation are bussers, servers, and chefs. (L.O. 19.9)

- When making forecasts based on daily tallies, managers should keep in mind that the number of customers served remains relatively constant from day to day during the week. (L.O. 19.10)

- The only way to determine hourly tallies is to have the dining room manager count and record the number of customers seated in the dining room every hour on the hour. (L.O. 19.10)

- Determining the number of employees required at various levels of business volume is typically based on historical records. (L.O. 19.10)

- Schedules for fixed-cost employees do not change from one week to the next. (L.O. 19.11)

- Determining the number of employees required at various levels of business volume so that an hourly schedule can be prepared is a technical, records-intensive process. (L.O. 19.12)

- Under normal circumstances, a test period of a particular number of days or weeks is established for gathering data in order to develop performance standards for fixed-cost personnel. (L.O. 19.13)

- Standard staffing requirements are traditionally known as performance criteria. (L.O. 19.14)

- The number of employee work hours required to perform a given volume of work is known as standard labor cost. (L.O. 19.14)

- There are limited opportunities for computer applications in establishing performance standards for labor. (L.O. 19.15)

Chapter 19 Check-in

1. The number of times a task can be performed within a certain time period is an example of a

   A. quantity standard.
   B. quality standard.
   C. cost standard.
   D. time and motion study.

   L.O. 19.1

2. The first step in establishing standards and standard procedures for employees is to

   A. hire employees.
   B. prepare job descriptions.
   C. schedule employees.
   D. organize the enterprise.

   L.O. 19.2

3. In an organization chart, the lines drawn from one position to another signify

   A. trainers and trainees.
   B. variable-cost personnel and fixed-cost personnel.
   C. lines of authority.
   D. wage levels.

   L.O. 19.4

4. Detailed written statements that describe jobs are known as

   A. job specifications.
   B. job analysis.
   C. performance standards.
   D. job descriptions.

   L.O. 19.5

5. The process of identifying the nature of a job, as well as the skills, level of education, and other specific qualifications needed to perform it, is called

   A. job analysis.
   B. job description.
   C. job specification.
   D. organizational planning.

   L.O. 19.6

6. Which part of the job description includes such information as the number of positions with that particular job title, the specific hours, and the supervisor to whom those with that job title report?

   A. List of specific job duties
   B. Heading
   C. Summary of job duties
   D. Organization chart

   L.O. 19.7

7. An increase or decrease in business volume will dictate the need for an increase or decrease in the number of which of the following employees?

   A. Managers
   B. Bookkeepers
   C. Chefs
   D. Servers

   L.O. 19.9

8. Which of the following is becoming the most common way to develop daily tallies?

    A. Use of electronic means to record sales
    B. Use of the Internet to gather data
    C. Use of sales history records to determine total number of covers
    D. Use of guest checks to determine total number of covers

L.O. 19.10

9. Working hours of which foodservice employees should be staggered to meet anticipated hourly demand?

    A. Fixed-cost employees
    B. Variable-cost employees
    C. Seasonal employees
    D. Part-time employees

L.O. 19.11

10. The amount of employee time required to perform a given volume of work is known as

    A. standard labor cost.
    B. standard staffing requirement.
    C. standard performance criteria.
    D. standard work hours.

L.O. 19.14

CHAPTER 20

Learning Objectives

20.1   Define *training*, and explain the difference between training and education.

20.2   Identify the objectives of training.

20.3   Explain the relationship of training needs assessment to the development of a training plan.

20.4   List and explain the ten elements commonly covered in a training plan.

20.5   Describe the advantages and disadvantages of centralized and local training for multi-unit organizations.

20.6   Identify the four content areas normally included in training manuals.

20.7   Describe two computer applications that can provide assistance to trainers.

Chapter 20 Study Outline

1. Training is narrowly focused on particular skills and tasks. It normally includes some education, but it is not the same as formal education.

2. The primary purpose of training is to improve job performance.

3. Most training plans include:

    - Objectives that identify the skills, tasks, and behaviors that a specific employee will have mastered by the time training is complete
    - Appropriate approaches to training (on-the-job or off-the-job, structured or unstructured, and individual or group)
    - Appropriate training methods (lecture/demonstration, role-playing, seminars, individual assignments, field trips, case studies, panels, and/or programmed instruction)
    - Instructional timetables
    - Appropriate location(s)
    - Lesson plans that include an objective, detailed notes about content, the instructional timetable, and any items that may be required during instruction
    - Trainer preparation
    - Trainee preparation
    - The training session, during which good trainers will respond to employees' questions, proceed at a reasonable pace, help trainees feel at ease, speak clearly, use words and phrases appropriate to the language level of the trainees, correct helpfully, and praise appropriately for good work
    - Evaluation

4. Many multi-unit companies have two choices available for any company-wide training program: send trainers to the individual units (localized training) or send trainees to a central training facility (centralized training).

5. Training manuals can be used any time that training is required, regardless of whether the training is done centrally or locally.

    - Training manuals may be written as guides for trainers or can give the trainee the information required, even if there is no trainer available to provide instruction.
    - Training manuals should include information that can be categorized into four areas: general background, specific duties of a job, specific procedures for carrying out the duties, and summary.

6. Programmed learning aids, interactive programs, and desktop publishing programs are just some examples of how computers can be used to train employees or create training manuals.

Chapter 20 Exercises

1. What is the difference between training and education?

   _____

   _____

   _____

   L.O. 20.1

2. What is the primary purpose of training?

   _____

   _____

   _____

   L.O. 20.2

3. Name three reasons to institute cross-training.

   • _____

   • _____

   • _____

   L.O. 20.3

4. Sunday's Bar and Grill is a 500-seat restaurant that includes an extensive lounge area with a front bar. Managers have hired a new bartender with very little experience.

   a. Which of the following would be the most appropriate training approach? Explain your choices.
      (1) On-the-job or off-the-job?

      _____

      _____

      _____

      (2) Structured or unstructured?

      _____

      _____

      _____

(3) Individual or group?

_____

_____

_____

   b. Which training method or combination of methods described in the text would be the most appropriate? Why?

_____

_____

_____

   c. Devise a lesson plan for training the new bartender.

_____

_____

_____

L.O. 20.3

5. Identify whether each of the follow refers to or describes localized training (L) or centralized training (C).

    _____a. Good choice when many in a single unit all require the same training

    _____b. Trainees sent to a training facility at the national or regional headquarters of the organization

    _____c. Trainers sent to individual units

    _____d. Good choice when many people at various locations all require the same training

L.O. 20.5

6. Name the four content areas usually included in a training manual.

- _____
- _____
- _____
- _____

L.O. 20.6

7. Name one computer application used in employee training.

_____

L.O. 20.7

Chapter 20 Check-in

1. The process by means of which individuals acquire the skills necessary to perform particular tasks is called
   A. crosstraining.
   B. the case study method.
   C. training.
   D. education.
L.O. 20.1

2. The primary purpose of training is to
   A. improve job performance.
   B. increase profits.
   C. decrease employee turnover.
   D. increase employee morale.
L.O. 20.2

3. A series of elements that constitute a method for teaching a specific employee the skills required to perform a job is called a
   A. seminar.
   B. panel.
   C. structured program.
   D. training plan.
L.O. 20.3

4. A new pot washer can best be trained
   A. in a group.
   B. through role playing.
   C. with programmed instruction.
   D. on the job.
L.O. 20.4

5. Which of the following works well in situations where high levels of skills training are not required?
   A. Unstructured training
   B. Off-the-job training
   C. Group training
   D. Localized training
L.O. 20.4

6. Which training method works best when preceded by more formal training delivered via one of the other methods?
   A. Role-playing
   B. Seminars
   C. Individual assignments
   D. Field trips
L.O. 20.4

7. Training locations should be determined by the
   A. nature of the training to be done.
   B. skills level of the trainee.
   C. particular job classifications of the trainees.
   D. trainer's background.
L.O. 20.4

8. Centralized training
    A. is a better choice when many individuals in a single unit all require the same training.
    B. is a better choice when many people in various locations all require the same training.
    C. requires that trainers be sent to individual units.
    D. is cost prohibitive for most small foodservice establishments.

L.O. 20.5

9. In which section of a training manual will the foodservice operation's principal goals and objectives be found?
    A. Summary
    B. Specific procedures for carrying out the duties of a job
    C. Specific duties of a job
    D. General background

L.O. 20.6

10. Programmed learning aids are often employed to provide employee training
    A. in a structured setting
    B. in group training sessions.
    C. on the premises.
    D. in remote locations.

L.O. 20.7

CHAPTER 21

MONITORING PERFORMANCE AND TAKING CORRECTIVE ACTION

Learning Objectives

21.1   Define the term *monitoring* as it is used in labor cost control.

21.2   Explain the difference between direct and indirect monitoring of employee performance.

21.3   Identify the two types of direct monitoring and provide examples of each.

21.4   List and describe four sources of information used for indirect monitoring.

21.5   Identify the five-step approach to identify the specific cause of some deviation between actual and standard performance.

21.6   List and describe the three general causes of discrepancies between actual performance and that anticipated by standards.

Chapter 21 Study Outline

1. To monitor the performance of employees is to gather information about their work and the results of that work.

    -   Employees' performance can be monitored directly, indirectly, or through a combination of the two.
    -   The sources that provide the information needed for indirect monitoring include customers, other employees, external groups (such as government agencies, chain organizations, food critics, and rating organizations), and managers.

2. If actual performance brings results that deviate significantly from those anticipated by established standards and standard procedures, some corrective action must be taken to bring actual performance in line with standards.

    - There is a generally accepted five-step approach that can be used to identify the cause of the deviation and find a suitable solution.
      (1) Meet with appropriate staff to point out the problem and determine its cause.
      (2) Identify all appropriate corrective measures that might be adopted.
      (3) Select the best corrective measure.
      (4) Institute the selected measure.
      (5) Monitor performance to be sure that the corrective measure has the desired effect.
    - There are three possible reasons for the discrepancy: inadequate performance, unsuitable standards, or inappropriate organization.
    - Reorganization sometimes results from the discovery of poor organization.
3. Many quick-service chains use computers to monitor servers' sales performance.

Chapter 21 Exercises

As the dining room supervisor of Venice Nights, you oversee many servers. Your ability to monitor them directly is limited.

1. Define monitoring in relation to the performance of your servers.

    _____

    _____

    _____

L.O. 21.1

2. Name two ways to accomplish direct monitoring and explain why direct monitoring would be difficult to implement at Venice Nights.

    - _____

    - _____

    _____

    _____

    _____

L.O. 21.2, 21.3

3. Explain the four ways managers can indirectly monitor employees. Provide specific examples.

- _____
  _____

- _____
  _____

- _____
  _____

- _____
  _____

L.O. 21.2, 21.4

4. Describe the five-step approach used to take corrective action when discrepancies between actual performance and standards/standard procedures are present.

- _____

- _____

- _____

- _____

- _____

L.O. 21.5

5. You have determined that there are three possible categories for discrepancies between the operation's standards and your servers' performance. Name the general categories and provide one example for each.

- _____
  _____

- _____
  _____

- _____
  _____

L.O. 21.6

Chapter 21 Check-in

1. Monitoring the performance of employees is which step in the control process?

   A. First
   B. Second
   C. Third
   D. Fourth

   L.O. 21.1

2. Examining the results of an employee's work and making a judgment about it immediately after it has been done is one type of

   A. indirect monitoring.
   B. direct monitoring.
   C. corrective action.
   D. differentiated observation.

   L.O. 21.2, 21.3

3. If restaurant customers feel the quality of food or service is low, they typically

   A. have little to say to dining room servers and supervisors.
   B. complain to management.
   C. walk out during the meal.
   D. return to the restaurant.

   L.O. 21.4

4. When reports about an employee come from coworkers, a supervisor must consider the reporting employee's

   A. status.
   B. salary.
   C. loyalty.
   D. motive.

   L.O. 21.4

5. Those who patronize restaurants and then inform the public about their professional views of the establishments are called

   A. food critics.
   B. OSHA inspectors.
   C. chain inspectors.
   D. spotters.

   L.O. 21.4

6. Once standards for work hours have been established, it becomes possible to

   A. conduct indirect monitoring by government agencies.
   B. make judgments about the number of actual work hours used in an establishment.
   C. create a budget.
   D. make promotion and termination decisions.

   L.O. 21.4

7. What is a possible reason for differences between standard work hours and actual hours worked?

   A. Lack of equipment or tools required
   B. Unforeseen variations in weather
   C. Need for additional training
   D. Inadequate compensation

   L.O. 21.4

8. What must occur before a manager can take corrective action?

   A. Meeting with appropriate staff to point out the problem and determine its cause
   B. Identifying all corrective measures that might be adopted
   C. Modifying standards and standard procedures
   D. Reviewing employee performance reports

L.O. 21.5

9. Which of the following is considered a possible reason for inadequate performance?

   A. Poor union/management relations
   B. Change of conditions, rendering standards inappropriate
   C. Increase in costs
   D. Decrease in sales

L.O. 21.6

10. A central difference between a temporary reduction of labor cost and a permanent reduction through reorganization typically involves the

    A. reason for the change.
    B. degree of change.
    C. potential savings.
    D. need for monitoring employee performance.

L.O. 21.6

Practice Test

This Practice Test contains 80 multiple-choice questions that are similar in content and format to those found on the National Restaurant Association Educational Foundation's final exam for this course. Mark the best answer to each question by circling the appropriate letter. Answers to the Practice Test are on page 143 of this Student Workbook.

1. As business volume increases, variable costs
   A. increase.
   B. decrease.
   C. remain constant.
   D. can no longer be tracked.
   L.O. 1.1, 1.2, 1.8

2. If a restaurant's total sales on a given day are $1,896 and 202 customers are served, what is the average sale per customer?
   A. $8.36
   B. $8.98
   C. $9.39
   D. $9.72
   L.O. 1.3

3. If the Uptown Grill's food costing $288,911 resulted in sales of $883,250, what was the establishment's cost percent for the year?
   A. 28.1%
   B. 32.7%
   C. 35.2%
   D. 36.0%
   L.O. 1.4, 1.5

4. Food cost percents tend to be relatively higher in which of the following types of foodservice establishments?
   A. Ethnic
   B. Gourmet
   C. Seafood
   D. Quick-service
   L.O. 1.6

5. Eliminating excessive costs for food, beverage, and labor is the ultimate goal of
   A. scheduling personnel.
   B. sales.
   C. variable rate.
   D. cost control.
   L.O. 2.1, 2.7

6. Which employee has the greatest control over the operation of a food and beverage establishment?
   A. Food controller
   B. Steward
   C. Manager
   D. Accountant
   L.O. 2.2

7. Standardized bowls, cups, and ladles are examples of which of the following standards?

   A. Quality
   B. Quantity
   C. Productivity
   D. Production

   L.O. 2.3

8. A realistic expression of management's goals and objectives expressed in financial terms is called a

   A. payback period.
   B. budget.
   C. standard cost.
   D. cost-benefit ratio.

   L.O. 2.3, 2.4, 2.7

9. Which of the following accurately represents the cost/volume/profit equation?

   A. $S = VC + CM + VR$
   B. $S = FC + CR + VR$
   C. $S = VC + FC + P$
   D. $S = FC + CR + CM$

   L.O. 3.2

10. If Vincent's Place has dollar sales of $999,000 and its variable costs are $443,556, which of the following is its variable rate?

    A. .444
    B. .544
    C. .554
    D. .614

    L.O. 3.2, 3.3

11. To determine an establishment's break-even point, a cost controller needs to

    A. calculate contribution margin.
    B. set profit to zero.
    C. examine historical records.
    D. multiply sales by variable cost.

    L.O. 3.1–3.3

12. Since variable costs at the Seafood Grill have not been effectively controlled, the establishment's variable rate has risen. Which of the following will directly result?

    A. Contribution rate will decrease.
    B. Profit will increase.
    C. Sales will decrease.
    D. Fixed costs will decrease.

    L.O. 3.1–3.3

13. Which of the following is a nonperishable food item?

    A Fruit yogurt
    B. Iceberg lettuce
    C. Ground turkey
    D. Ground pepper

    L.O. 4.2

14. Procedures for determining the appropriate purchase quantity for each item to be purchased are based primarily on which of the following?

    A. Par stock
    B. Useful life of the commodity
    C. Desired frequency of ordering
    D. Purveyors' minimum order requirements

    L.O. 4.4

15. A bin card tells managers
    A. how many entrees were rejected by customers.
    B. how much to order.
    C. the amount of an item on hand.
    D. how many portions have been sold.
    L.O. 4.7

16. The Early Morning Bakery delivers 10 loaves of bread to the Midtown Sandwich Shop every day. This arrangement is called a
    A. standing order.
    B. centralized purchasing system.
    C. route delivery.
    D. daily drop-off.
    L.O. 4.15

17. Foods that are categorized as directs are those that are
    A. charged immediately to cost.
    B. charged to cost when issued from inventory.
    C. verified against a purchase order.
    D. verified against an invoice.
    L.O. 5.9

18. Which of the following are printed on heavy card stock for durability and perforated into two parts for convenient separation?
    A. Menus
    B. Invoices
    C. Bin cards
    D. Meat tags
    L.O. 5.3–5.5, 5.10

19. While the food controller still has the receiving sheet, the important total figure he or she must record is the
    A. total cost of directs.
    B. unit cost of stores.
    C. contribution margin.
    D. turnover rate.
    L.O. 5.3

20. When receiving employees become lax in their duties, which of the following is required until they have improved their performance to the desired extent?
    A. Demotion
    B. Frequent monitoring
    C. Group training sessions
    D. Incentives
    L.O. 5.12

21. For perishable foods, shelving should be slatted in order to
    A. protect them from insects and vermin.
    B. permit maximum circulation of air in refrigerated facilities.
    C. prevent the accumulation of small amounts of spoiling food.
    D. ensure that older quantities are used before any new deliveries.
    L.O. 6.2, 6.4

22. A form filled in by a member of the kitchen staff listing the items and quantities the kitchen staff needs from stores for the current day's production is called a(n)
    A. requisition.
    B. FIFO.
    C. request form.
    D. usage request.
    L.O. 6.6

23. Multiplying the unit value of each meat or entree item by the number of units issued is called

   A. extrapolating.
   B. pilferage.
   C. record keeping.
   D. extending the requisition.

   L.O. 6.7

24. The bartender at Hal & Edie's has secured some oranges, lemons, and limes from the kitchen for use in a number of specialty drinks. This transfer is classified as

   A. interunion.
   B. intraunit.
   C. interunit.
   D. internal.

   L.O. 6.10

25. In what way are frozen green beans likely to be quantified?

   A. By weight
   B. By volume
   C. By count
   D. By capacity

   L.O. 7.1

26. Which of the following help to establish consistency of taste, appearance, and customer acceptance?

   A. Standard portion costs
   B. Standard recipes
   C. Standard portion sizes
   D. Portion cost factors

   L.O. 7.1

27. Which of the following is used to determine standard portion cost for an item to be divided into portions after cooking?

   A. Formula
   B. Recipe detail and cost card
   C. Butcher test
   D. Cooking loss test

   L.O. 7.2

28. Approximately how many pounds of beef tenderloin should a steward buy if he or she wants to provide six-ounce portions to 35 people and has calculated a yield percentage of 42.6%?

   A. 18
   B. 31
   C. 35
   D. 52

   L.O. 7.5

29. Which of the following is typically used to manually maintain sales histories?

   A. Guest checks
   B. Portion sales breakdowns
   C. Point of sale terminals
   D. Calendars of special events

   L.O. 8.2, 8.3

30. Of the 1,325 portion sold at Danny's Grill last week, 525 were hamburgers. What is the popularity index for this item?

   A. 31.2%
   B. 39.6%
   C. 42.1%
   D. 48.1%

   L.O. 8.6

31. Which of the following translates management's portion sales forecasts into production targets?

    A. Production sheet
    B. Production budget
    C. Production inventory record
    D. Void sheet

L.O. 8.8

32. Information about returned portions is recorded on a(n)

    A. portion inventory and reconciliation sheet.
    B. production sheet.
    C. excessive cost record.
    D. void sheet.

L.O. 8.9

33. The method used for determining the value of a physical inventory that assigns the earliest prices paid for units is the

    A. first-in, first-out.
    B. weighted average purchase price.
    C. actual purchase price.
    D. last-in, first-out.

L.O. 9.3, 9.5

34. If cost of food sold is $10,000 and sales are $20,000, what is the food cost percent?

    A. 0.5%
    B. 5%
    C. 50%
    D. 200%

L.O. 9.10

35. Grease sales are

    A. added to cost of food issued.
    B. subtracted from cost of food issued.
    C. multiplied by cost of food issued.
    D. added to cost of food sold.

L.O. 9.4, 9.6

36. A primary advantage of the daily or weekly food cost report is that it

    A. is easier to prepare than the monthly food cost report.
    B. can be prepared quickly.
    C. allows management to make weekly or daily operating decisions.
    D. reduces variable rate.

L.O. 9.11

37. Which of the following can be calculated to help overcome the problem of artificially high food cost percent one day and low food cost percent the next?

    A. Cost of stores
    B. Total sales
    C. Food cost percent to date
    D. Transfers and other adjustments

L.O. 10.1, 10.2

38. Figures for food cost, food sales, and food cost percent for any one specific day and for all the days to date in the period are compared to those for a similar period of a

    A. closing inventory report.
    B. budget.
    C. menu precost and abstract.
    D. daily report.

L.O. 10.3

39. The value of closing inventory based on records and indicating purchases and issues is called

  A. physical inventory.
  B. opening inventory.
  C. book inventory.
  D. realized inventory.
L.O. 10.4

40. On a menu pre-cost and abstract form, if the number of portions forecasted for the spaghetti meal is 70, the standard portion cost is $2.95, and the sales price is $8.50, what is the total cost for the item?

  A. $206.50
  B. $382.75
  C. $453.50
  D. $595.00
L.O. 11.2

41. The cost percent calculated on the abstract side of the menu pre-cost and abstract indicates

  A. the number of portion sales forecasted for each menu item.
  B. what the cost percent should have been if everything had gone according to plan.
  C. the prices reflected on an operation's menu.
  D. total standard costs.
L.O. 11.2

42. The difference between actual costs and standard costs is known as

  A. deviation.
  B. excessive cost.
  C. potential savings.
  D. standard discrepancy.
L.O. 11.3

43. To the extent that savings can be achieved without incurring other costs, which of the following will increase?

  A. Food cost
  B. Forecasted sales
  C. Actual cost percent
  D. Profits
L.O. 11.5

44. Which of the following is not generally a goal of sales control?

  A. Profit maximization
  B. Menu analysis
  C. Revenue control
  D. Sales optimization.
L.O. 12.1

45. Other factors being equal, customers will usually choose

  A. a homogeneous product or service.
  B. a differentiated product or service.
  C. the daily special.
  D. the most conveniently located restaurant.
L.O. 12.2

46. Which of the following is considered an "equitable" pricing method, with each customer bearing only his fair share of the costs and profits?

  A. Matching competitors' prices
  B. Calculating prices from costs and cost percents
  C. Adding desired contribution margins to portion costs
  D. Employing menu analysis
L.O. 12.4

47. The dupe system is a
    A. training program for food servers.
    B. sales technique used to induce customers to ask for items that they might not otherwise consider ordering.
    C. method of recording customers' orders that provides two copies of each order.
    D. way to turn "plowhorses" into "stars."
L.O. 12.9, 12.10

48. A natural process resulting from the addition of yeast to a liquid containing malted grain and hops is called
    A. distillation.
    B. fermentation.
    C. condensation.
    D. substantiation.
L.O. 13.4

49. An alcoholic beverage described as 40 proof is what percent alcohol?
    A. 20%
    B. 40%
    C. 80%
    D. 120%
L.O. 13.5

50. A customer who orders a "rum and Coke" will be given which of the following?
    A. Generic brand of alcohol
    B. Call brand
    C. Pouring brand
    D. Mixer
L.O. 13.6

51. With respect to processing beverage orders, it is advisable to establish a purchasing routine that
    A. is simple and straightforward.
    B. requires coordinated efforts from both employees and managers.
    C. is not time-consuming.
    D. requires formal written purchase orders.
L.O. 13.12

52. In the context of storing beverages, in order to prevent pilferage, it is necessary to
    A. hire honest employees.
    B. make all beverage storage areas secure.
    C. provide storeroom employees with adequate training.
    D. administer lie-detector tests on a regular basis.
L.O. 14. 1, 14.2

53. The use of bin cards enables a wine steward to
    A. maintain a perpetual inventory record of quantities on hand.
    B. prevent the theft of expensive alcoholic beverages.
    C. maximize shelf life of stored beverages.
    D. lower inventory costs.
L.O. 14.6

54. The degree of moisture in the air is of significance only for those beverages purchased in
    A. corked bottles.
    B. large quantities.
    C. control states.
    D. kegs.
L.O. 14.7

55. Establishments that operate more than one bar must
    A. employ closed-circuit television in order to monitor employee performance.
    B. use indelible ink to code bottles.
    C. prepare separate requisitions for each.
    D. hire substantially more employees than they would otherwise.
L.O. 14.10

56. A device fitted on top of a bottle of alcohol that measures the quantity poured from the bottle is called a
    A. shot glass.
    B. jigger.
    C. free-pouring device.
    D. pourer.
L.O. 15.3

57. Which of the following makes it possible for a bartender to prepare various unusual drinks that are requested only on rare occasions?
    A. Book of standard recipes
    B. Standard procedures
    C. Automated dispensers
    D. Standard recipe detail and cost card
L.O. 15.5

58. If the purchase price of a bottle of gin is $17.85 and the bottle contains 16.5 drinks, what is the standard cost of each drink?
    A. $0.64
    B. $0.83
    C. $1.08
    D. $1.32
L.O. 15.6

59. Which of the following is added to the cost of liquor consumed?
    A. Cooking liquor
    B. Officers' drinks
    C. Special promotions
    D. Mixers
L.O. 16.2

60. The difference between the sales price of a given drink and the sales value of its primary ingredient if sold as a straight shot is know as the
    A. turnover rate.
    B. average sales value.
    C. mixed drink differential.
    D. potential sales value.
L.O. 16.8

61. Which beverage monitoring method has been resuscitated with the increasing use of computers for beverage control?
    A. Cost control approach
    B. Inventory method
    C. Ounce-control method
    D. Actual sales record method
L.O. 16.13

62. The popularity of drinks with lower alcohol content helps explain the
    A. goals of beverage sales control.
    B. incidental nature of drinking.
    C. difference between actual and standard beverage costs.
    D. focus on low-calorie substitutes.
L.O. 17.2

63. Late-afternoon clientele of office workers looking for moderately priced, large drinks made with high-quality liquor can be described as a

A. market segment.
B. guest group.
C. popularity index.
D. plowhorse.

L.O. 17.3

64. In beverage operations, profit maximization cannot be accomplished by

A. establishing drink prices that will maximize gross profit.
B. influencing customers' selections.
C. increasing customer purchases.
D. posting appealing photographs of specialty house drinks.

L.O. 17.4, 17.5

65. Which technique is sometimes adopted by bartenders who selectively overpour?

A. Undercharging
B. Overcharging
C. Diluting bottle contents
D. Underpouring

L.O. 17.6

66. What are the two forms of current compensation commonly received by employees in the hospitality industry?

A. Direct and indirect
B. Salary and wages
C. Wages and tips
D. Salary and pension benefits

L.O. 18.1

67. Bonuses and commissions are examples of which of the following?

A. Direct compensation
B. Indirect compensation
C. Deferred compensation
D. Future compensation

L.O. 18.1, 18.2

68. Employers can often pay comparatively lower hourly rates, thereby keeping labor costs down, in operations

A. with modern equipment.
B. in rural areas.
C. that outsource.
D. with competent management.

L.O. 18.3, 18.4

69. Labor cost control can be achieved by

A. employing a bare minimum number of people paid the minimum legal wage.
B. employing unskilled employees and training them appropriately.
C. directing and regulating employees' actions to obtain desired levels of performance at appropriate levels of cost.
D. initiating short-term policies geared to minimizing immediate costs.

L.O. 18.5, 18.6

70. The majority of foodservice operations are not able to use

A. organizational plans.
B. assembly line techniques.
C. daily tallies.
D. standard labor cost.

L.O. 19.2

71. Statements that describe an acceptable level of job performance are known as
    A. standard staffing requirements.
    B. medians.
    C. performance criteria.
    D. job specifications.
L.O. 19.5

72. Which of the following outlines the qualifications needed to perform a job?
    A. Job specification
    B. Job analysis
    C. Job description
    D. Organization chart
L.O. 19.8

73. If three dishwashers are needed over a three hour shift, how many work hours are required to perform this specified volume of work?
    A. 3
    B. 5
    C. 6
    D. 9
L.O. 19.14

74. The primary purpose of training is to
    A. convey information to new employees.
    B. improve job performance.
    C. increase productivity.
    D. allow employees to share their opinions and concerns.
L.O. 20.2

75. Which training method is excellent for teaching specific skills?
    A. Role playing
    B. Seminars
    C. Case studies
    D. Panels
L.O. 20.4

76. Which of the following is a good choice when many individuals in various locations all require the same training?
    A. Localized training
    B. Centralized training
    C. Structured training
    D. Unstructured training
L.O. 20.5

77. Gathering information about the work of an employee and the results of that work is called
    A. investigation.
    B. performance monitoring.
    C. record keeping.
    D. periodic control.
L.O. 21.1

78. The extent to which direct monitoring can take place is dependent on the
    A. monitoring skills of the supervisor.
    B. layout of the foodservice establishment.
    C. number of employees working under the jurisdiction of a supervisor.
    D. goals of the foodservice operation.
L.O. 21.3

79. Learning about employee performance through customers is one form of

    A. networking.
    B. direct monitoring.
    C. indirect monitoring.
    D. goodwill.

L.O. 21.2, 21.4

80. The initial difficulty in taking corrective action lies in

    A. scheduling meetings with appropriate staff to point out problems.
    B. determining all appropriate corrective measures that may be adopted.
    C. putting together a reorganization team.
    D. identifying the reasons for discrepancies.

L.O. 21.5

Practice Test Answer Key

1.	A	p. 9	28.	B	p. 171	55.	C	p. 351
2.	C	p. 14	29.	A	p. 183	56.	D	p. 363
3.	B	p. 17	30.	B	p. 187	57.	A	p. 367
4.	D	pp. 21–22	31.	A	p. 190	58.	C	p. 370
5.	D	p. 33	32.	D	p. 195	59.	D	p. 389
6.	C	p. 34	33.	D	p. 211	60.	C	p. 399
7.	B	p. 37	34.	C	p. 214	61.	C	p. 397
8.	B	p. 44	35.	B	p. 215	62.	B	p. 417
9.	C	p. 65	36.	C	p. 222	63.	A	p. 419
10.	A	p. 68	37.	C	p. 236	64.	D	p. 420
11.	B	p. 69	38.	D	p. 238	65.	C	p. 424
12.	A	p. 69	39.	C	p. 242	66.	A	pp. 434–435
13.	D	p. 86	40.	A	p. 260	67.	A	p. 435
14.	B	p. 89	41.	B	p. 255	68.	B	p. 443
15.	C	p. 94	42.	C	p. 256	69.	C	p. 450
16.	A	p. 106	43.	D	p. 261	70.	B	p. 458
17.	A	p. 116	44.	B	p. 269	71.	C	p. 463
18.	D	p. 118	45.	D	p. 270	72.	A	p. 466
19.	A	p. 119	46.	C	p. 280	73.	D	pp. 476–477
20.	B	pp. 121–122	47.	C	p. 293	74.	B	p. 490
21.	B	p. 128	48.	B	p. 313	75.	A	p. 496
22.	A	p. 132	49.	A	p. 317	76.	B	p. 504
23.	D	p. 135	50.	C	p. 320	77.	B	p. 510
24.	B	p. 138	51.	D	p. 327	78.	C	p. 511
25.	A	p. 153	52.	B	p. 342	79.	C	p. 511
26.	B	p. 155	53.	A	pp. 344–345	80.	D	p. 520
27.	D	p. 161	54.	A	p. 347			

Chapter Check-In Answer Keys

Chapter 1

1.	C	pp. 7–8	5.	D	p. 14	9.	B	p. 22
2.	B	p. 8	6.	B	p. 16	10.	D	p. 24
3.	A	p. 10	7.	A	p. 17			
4.	C	p. 12	8.	A	p. 20			

Chapter 2

1.	A	p. 33	5.	D	p. 42	9.	C	p. 55
2.	B	p. 34	6.	A	p. 44	10.	C	p. 55
3.	C	p. 37	7.	B	p. 50			
4.	D	p. 41	8.	C	p. 51			

Chapter 3

1.	B	p. 63	5.	B	p. 69	9.	D	pp. 71–72
2.	B	p. 65	6.	D	pp. 69–71	10.	C	p. 72
3.	C	p. 65	7.	A	p. 71			
4.	C	p. 68	8.	C	p. 69			

Chapter 4

1.	C	p. 86	5.	B	p. 94	9.	D	p. 105
2.	C	p. 87	6.	C	p. 97	10.	A	p. 106
3.	D	p. 89	7.	D	p. 100			
4.	A	pp. 92–93	8.	C	p. 101			

Chapter 5

1.	B	p. 112	5.	A	p. 115	9.	D	p. 121
2.	A	p. 112	6.	D	p. 117	10.	A	pp. 117–118
3.	D	p. 119	7.	C	p. 117			
4.	D	p. 121	8.	A	p. 119			

Chapter 6

1.	C	p. 130	5.	A	p. 132	9.	A	p. 140
2.	B	p. 127	6.	B	p. 134	10.	B	p. 142
3.	A	p. 128	7.	C	p. 136			
4.	D	p. 129	8.	D	p. 137			

Chapter 7

1.	A	p. 152	5.	A	p. 159	8.	C	p. 171
2.	B	p. 153	6.	C	pp. 162–163	9.	D	p. 174
3.	B	p. 155	7.	C	pp. 164–165	10.	D	p. 175
4.	B	p. 158						

Chapter 8

1.	A	p. 182	5.	A	pp. 187–188	9.	C	p. 200
2.	A	p. 183	6.	C	pp. 189–190	10.	A	p. 200
3.	A	p. 185	7.	B	p. 190			
4.	C	p. 187	8.	D	p. 196			

Chapter 9

1.	D	p. 206	5.	C	p. 211	9.	B	p. 220
2.	B	p. 207	6.	D	p. 214	10.	A	p. 223
3.	D	p. 208	7.	C	p. 215			
4.	B	p. 210	8.	A	p. 217			

Chapter 10

1.	A	p. 234	5.	A	p. 239	9.	C	pp. 243–244
2.	C	p. 234	6.	B	p. 241	10.	A	p. 245
3.	C	p. 235	7.	B	p. 242			
4.	D	p. 236	8.	B	p. 243			

Chapter 11

1.	B	p. 250	5.	B	p. 253	9.	D	p. 261
2.	B	p. 251	6.	A	p. 256	10.	D	p. 262
3.	C	p. 252	7.	B	p. 256			
4.	B	p. 253	8.	D	p. 260			

Chapter 12

1.	A	p. 268	5.	D	p. 280	9.	B	p. 290
2.	B	p. 272	6.	C	p. 282	10.	B	p. 296
3.	C	p. 276	7.	B	p. 285			
4.	D	p. 278	8.	A	p. 287			

Chapter 13

1.	A	p. 313	5.	A	p. 320	9.	C	pp. 323–324
2.	C	p. 314	6.	B	p. 322	10.	C	p. 331
3.	B	p. 315	7.	B	p. 324			
4.	D	p. 317	8.	D	p. 322			

Chapter 14

1.	D	p. 338	5.	A	p. 343	9.	C	p. 349
2.	A	p. 349	6.	D	p. 345	10.	B	p. 353
3.	A	p. 339	7.	B	p. 347			
4.	A	p. 340	8.	B	p. 349			

Chapter 15

1. C   p. 360
2. D   p. 370
3. B   p. 363
4. A   p. 365
5. B   p. 367
6. C   p. 370
7. D   pp. 376–377
8. A   p. 377
9. B   p. 379
10. A   p. 380

Chapter 16

1. C   p. 397
2. D   p. 387
3. D   p. 388
4. C   p. 391
5. A   p. 395
6. B   p. 396
7. B   pp. 398, 399
8. B   p. 401
9. A   p. 403
10. D   p. 407

Chapter 17

1. A   p. 417
2. B   p. 417
3. C   p. 419
4. B   p. 420
5. A   p. 421
6. B   p. 423
7. B   p. 425
8. B   p. 426
9. C   p. 427
10. D   p. 428

Chapter 18

1. C   p. 434
2. B   p. 435
3. C   p. 435
4. C   p. 437
5. C   p. 439
6. C   pp. 439–440
7. D   p. 441
8. C   p. 447
9. D   p. 450
10. D   p. 450

Chapter 19

1. A   p. 457
2. D   p. 459
3. C   p. 460
4. D   p. 463
5. A   p. 462
6. B   p. 464
7. D   p. 467
8. A   p. 469
9. B   p. 476
10. D   p. 482

Chapter 20

1. C   p. 490
2. A   p. 490
3. D   p. 492
4. D   pp. 493, 494
5. A   pp. 494–495
6. C   pp. 496–497
7. A   pp. 499–500
8. B   p. 504
9. D   p. 505
10. C   p. 506

Chapter 21

1. C   p. 510
2. B   p. 510
3. A   pp. 511–512
4. D   p. 513
5. A   p. 515
6. B   p. 517
7. B   p. 519
8. A   p. 520
9. A   p. 520
10. B   p. 522